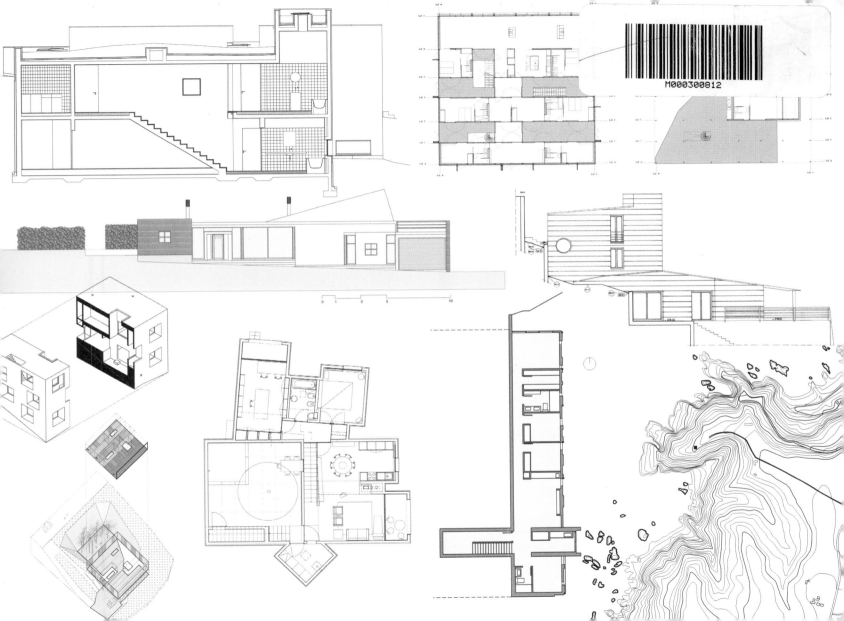

0 1   3   5   10

HOUSE PLANS
for Challenging Sites

© 2019 Instituto Monsa de ediciones.

First edition in 2019 by Monsa Publications,
an imprint of Monsa Publications Gravina 43
(08930) Sant Adrià de Besós. Barcelona (Spain)
T +34 93 381 00 50
www.monsa.com monsa@monsa.com

Editor and Project Director Anna Minguet
Art director & layout Eva Minguet
(Monsa Publications)
Printed by Cachiman Gràfic

Shop online:
www.monsashop.com

Follow us!
Instagram: @monsapublications
Facebook: @monsashop

ISBN: 978-84-17557-02-7
D.L. B 6911-2019
March 2019

HOUSE PLANS
for Challenging Sites

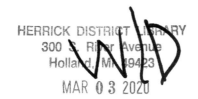

INTRO

House Plans for Challenging Sites features more than 350 floor plans, sections, sketches, and elevations, as well as construction details of 35 housing projects which represent a true challenge for architects, either because of their topography or the geological composition of the soil. Secluded, hard-to-reach locations, as well as sloping terrains, make it necessary to innovate when it comes to organizing and planning structures. In many projects, air currents, sunshine hours, and pluviometry have been taken into account as these elements determine the subsequent inclusion of energy-efficiency-enhancing systems – rainwater collection and reuse tanks, or the location of openings and courtyards, which allows for an optimal use of breeze in order to cool down homes in a natural fashion. Regarding their outside appearance, these homes are designed to integrate into the landscape and minimize environmental impact, since they are mostly located in beautiful, ecologically diverse natural settings.

House Plans for Challenging Sites contiene más de 350 planos de plantas, secciones, bocetos y alzados, así como detalles constructivos de un total de 35 proyectos de viviendas que ya sea por su topografía o por la composición geológica del terreno, suponen un verdadero reto para los arquitectos. La ubicación apartada y de difícil acceso o el desnivel del terreno, lleva a innovar en la organización y la planificación de las estructuras. En muchos de los proyectos se han tenido en cuenta aspectos como las corrientes de aire, las horas de sol y la pluviometría. Estos elementos marcan la posterior inclusión de sistemas que mejoran la eficiencia energética de las casas: depósitos para recoger y reutilizar el agua de la lluvia, o la situación de las aberturas y de los patios, que permite aprovechar las brisas para refrigerar las casas de forma natural. Exteriormente, son casas que quieren integrarse en el paisaje y minimizar cualquier alteración del entorno, al tratarse en su mayoría de paisajes naturales de gran belleza y diversidad ecológica.

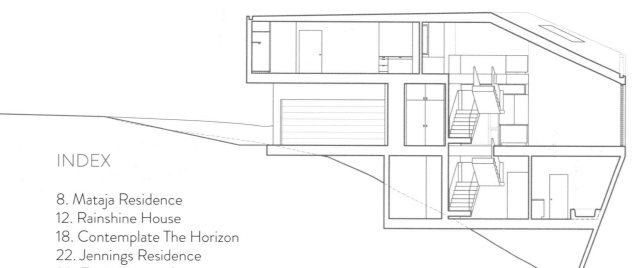

INDEX

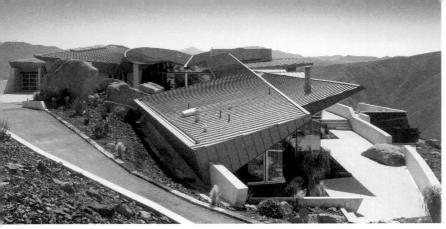

Mataja Residence

Belzberg Architects
Santa Monica Mountains, CA, USA
Photos © Tim Street-Porter

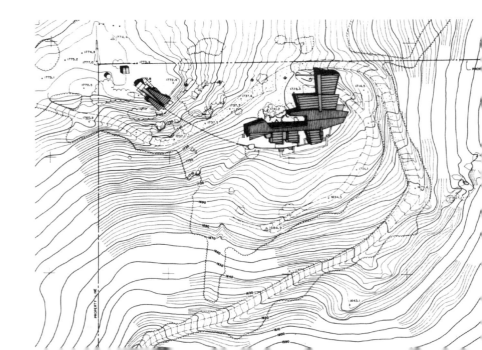

Site plan

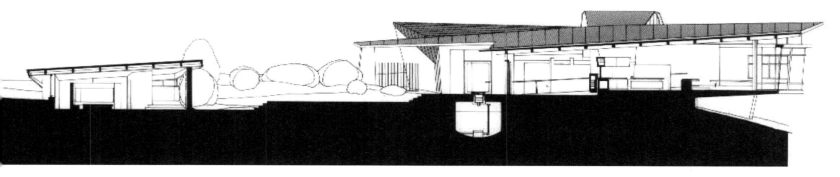

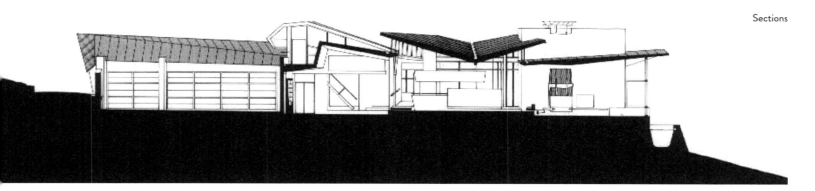

Sections

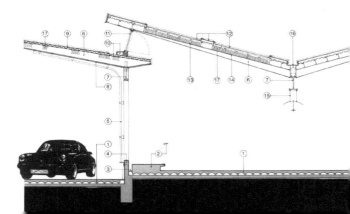

Constructive detail

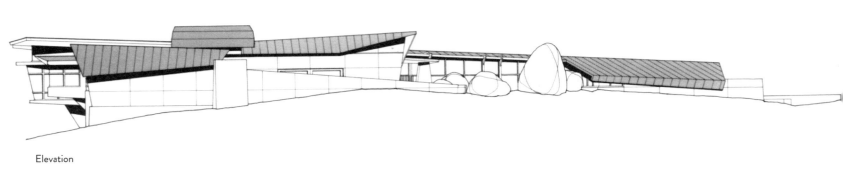

Elevation

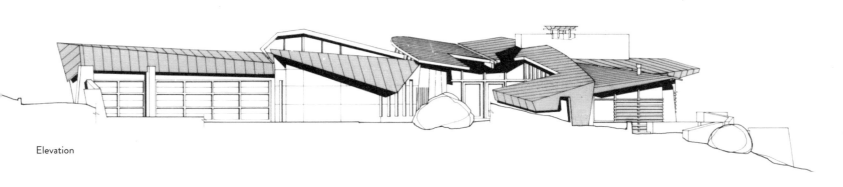

Elevation

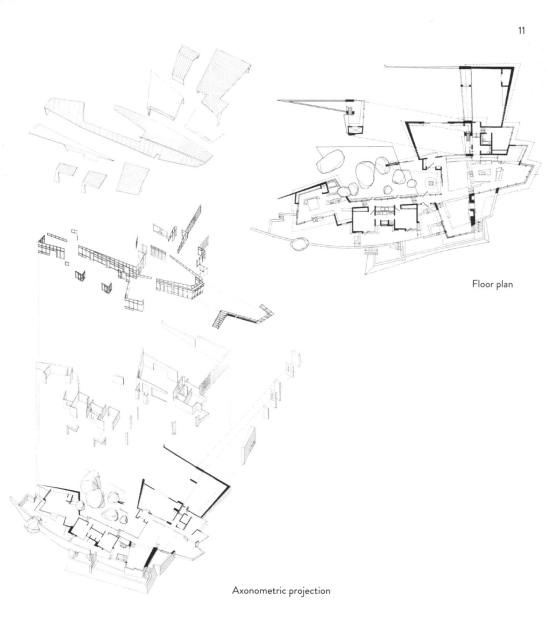

Floor plan

Axonometric projection

Rainshine House

Robert M. Cain, Architect, AIA, Leed AP
Decatur, GA, USA
Photos © Paul Hultberg

Site plan
1. House
2. Covered deck
3. Screened porch
4. Entry
5. Photovoltaic array
6. Concrete SLAB
7. Landscaping steps
8. Rain garden
9. Community Path
10. Wheel strips

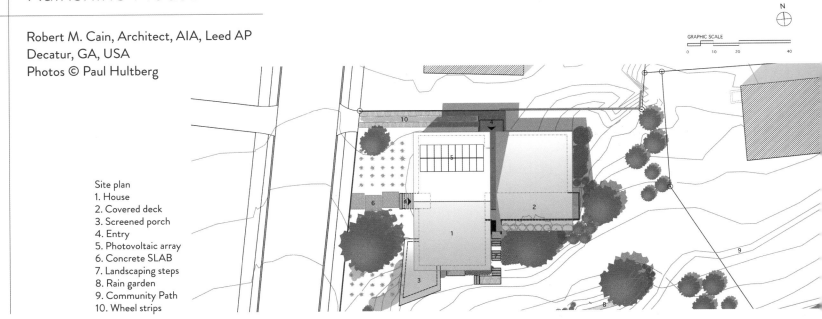

GRAPHIC SCALE
0   10   20   40

N

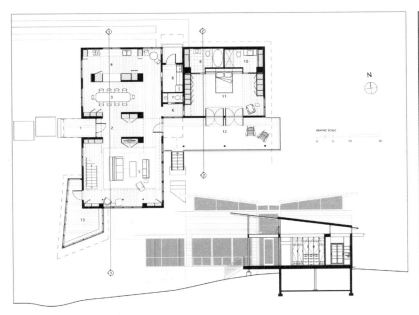

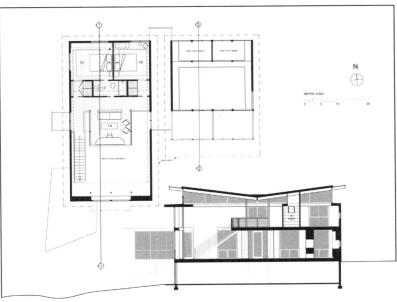

First floor plan and section 2-2
1. Entry
2. Lobby
3. Dining room
4. Kitchen
5. Living room
6. Corridor
7. 1/2 Bath
8. Laundry
9. Her master bath
10. His master bath
11. Master bedroom
12. Covered deck
13. Screened porch

Second floor plan and section 1-1
14. Office loft
15. Bedroom
16. Guest bedroom
17. Bathroom

Star elevation (scale: 1/4"=1'-0")

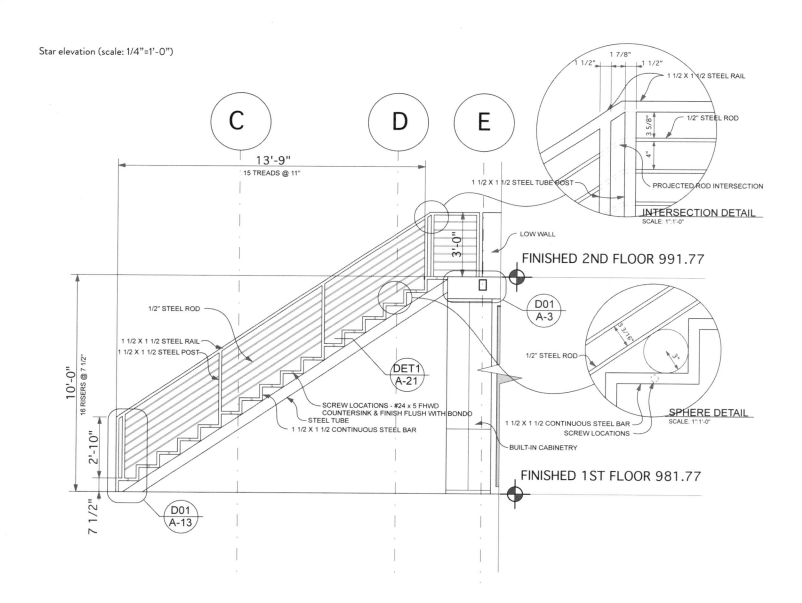

C   D   E

13'-9"
15 TREADS @ 11"

1 1/2 X 1 1/2 STEEL TUBE POST

1 1/2" 1 7/8" 1 1/2"

1 1/2 X 1 1/2 STEEL RAIL

1/2" STEEL ROD

3 5/8"

4"

PROJECTED ROD INTERSECTION

INTERSECTION DETAIL
SCALE: 1":1'-0"

3'-0"

LOW WALL

FINISHED 2ND FLOOR 991.77

1/2" STEEL ROD

1 1/2 X 1 1/2 STEEL RAIL
1 1/2 X 1 1/2 STEEL POST

DET1
A-21

D01
A-3

3 3/16"

3"

1/2" STEEL ROD

SPHERE DETAIL
SCALE: 1":1'-0"

SCREW LOCATIONS - #24 x 5 FHWD
COUNTERSINK & FINISH FLUSH WITH BONDO
STEEL TUBE
1 1/2 X 1 1/2 CONTINUOUS STEEL BAR

1 1/2 X 1 1/2 CONTINUOUS STEEL BAR
SCREW LOCATIONS

BUILT-IN CABINETRY

FINISHED 1ST FLOOR 981.77

10'-0"
16 RISERS @ 7 1/2"

2'-10"

7 1/2"

D01
A-13

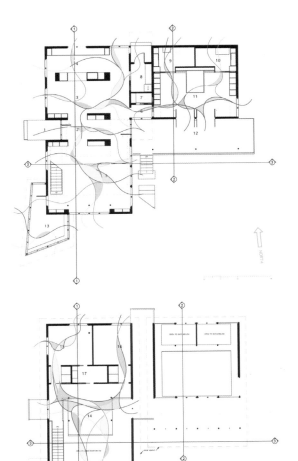

First floor plan
1. Entry
2. Lobby
3. Dining room
4. Kitchen
5. Living room
6. Corridor
7. 1/2 Bath
8. Laundry
9. Her master bath
10. His master bath
11. Master bedroom
12. Covered deck
13. Screened porch

Second floor plan
14. Office loft
15. Bedroom
16. Guest bedroom
17. Bathroom

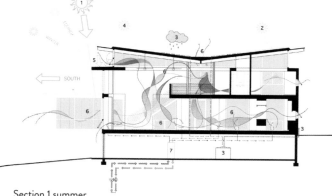

Section 1 summer
1. Summer noon sun
2. Photovoltaic array facing south for maximum solar exposure
3. Rainwater collection from roof, pumped to landscape and toilet use
4. High albedo surface reflects solar heat from absorbing into roofing material
5. Overhangs and light shelves shadoow high summer sun and refract indirect light into the interior
6. Open floor plan, connecting porch, low operable windows, high celing fans and operable clerestory windows createa crossvventilation and stack effect
7. Geo-thermal heat pump for supplementary cooling

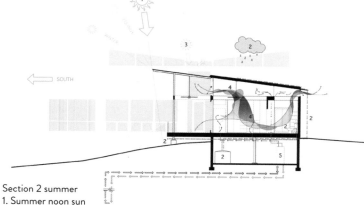

Section 2 summer
1. Summer noon sun
2. Rainwater collection from roof, pumped to landscape and toilet use
3. High albedo surface reflects solar heat from absorbing into roofing material
4. Open floor plan, connecting porch, low operable windows, large screened doors, high ceiling fans and operable clerestory windows create croos ventilation and stack effect
5. Geo-thermal heat pump for supplementary cooling

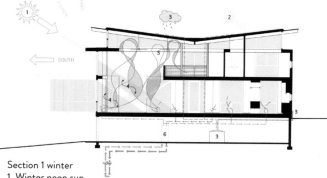

Section 1 winter
1. Winter noon sun
2. Photovoltaic array facing south for maximum solar exposure
3. Rainwater collection from roof, pumped to landscape and toilet use
4. Solar heat gain from large southern windows
5. High ceiling fans circulate heated air through clerestory space
6. Geo-thermal heat pump for supplementary heating

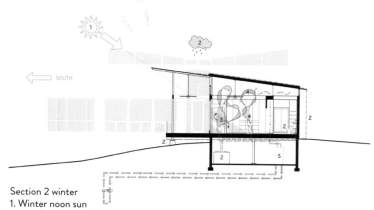

Section 2 winter
1. Winter noon sun
2. Rainwater collection from roof, pumped to landscape and toilet use
3. Solar heat gain from large southern windows
4. High ceiling fans circulate heated air through clerestory space
5. Geo-thermal heat pump for supplementary heating

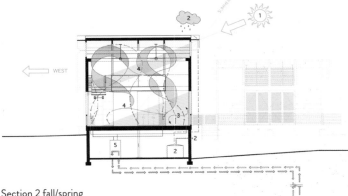

Section 2 fall/spring
1. Fall/spring 9am sun
2. Rainwater collection from butterfly roof, pumped to landscape and toilet use
3. Solar heat gain
4. Open floor plan and high fans circulate heated air
5. Rainshine does not rely on geo-thermal heat pump to heat house in cool morning temperatures

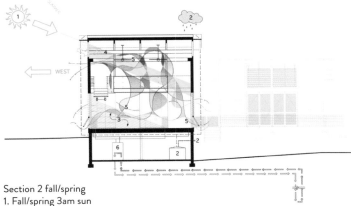

Section 2 fall/spring
1. Fall/spring 3am sun
2. Rainwater collection from butterfly roof, pumped to landscape and toilet use
3. Solar heat gain is greatly reduced by the use of large semi-opaque roller shades
4. Light shelves shadow high sun and refract indirect light into the interior
5. Open floor plan, connecting porch, low operable windows, high ceiling fans and operable clerestory windows circulate air and create cross ventilation and a stack effect
6. Rainshine does not rely on geo-thermal heat pump to cool the house in hot afternoon temperatures

Contemplate The Horizon

Arquiprojecta
Santarem, Portugal
Photos © Fernando Guerra / FG+SG

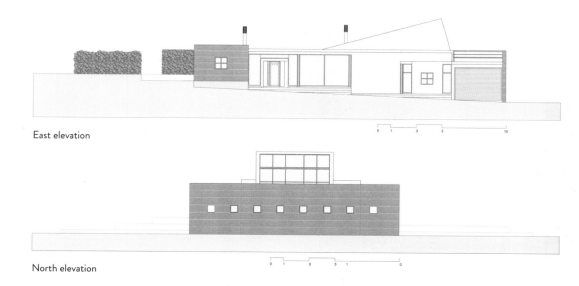

East elevation

North elevation

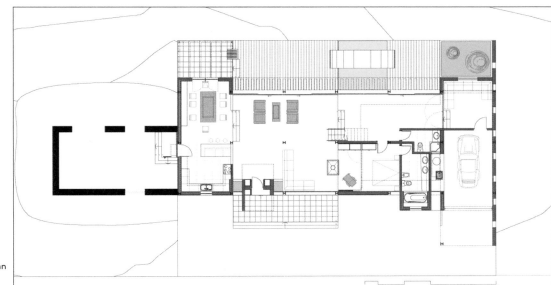

Lower floor plan

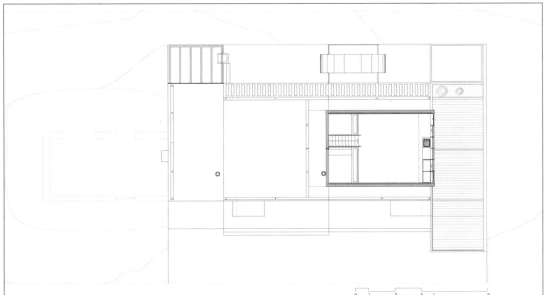

Upper floor plan

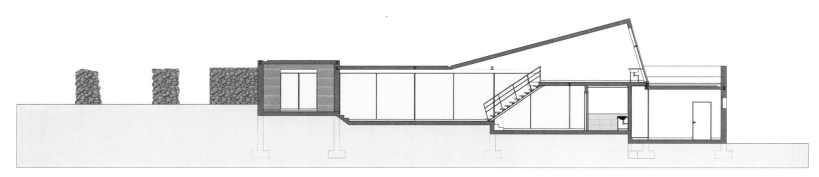

Section 1

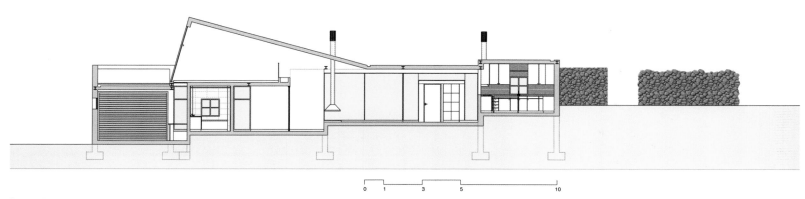

Section 2

0 1   3   5   10

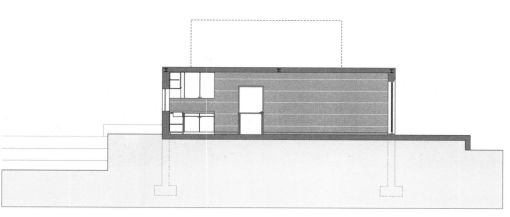

Section 3

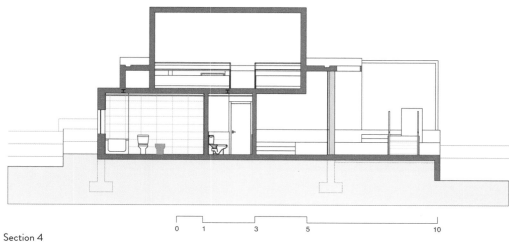

Section 4

0   1   3   5   10

Jennings Residence

Workroom Design
Hopkins Point, Warranambool, Australia
Photos © Trevor Mein/Meinphoto

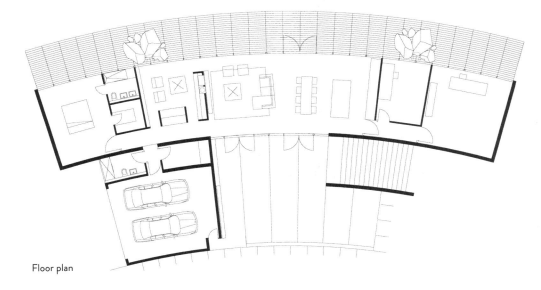

Floor plan

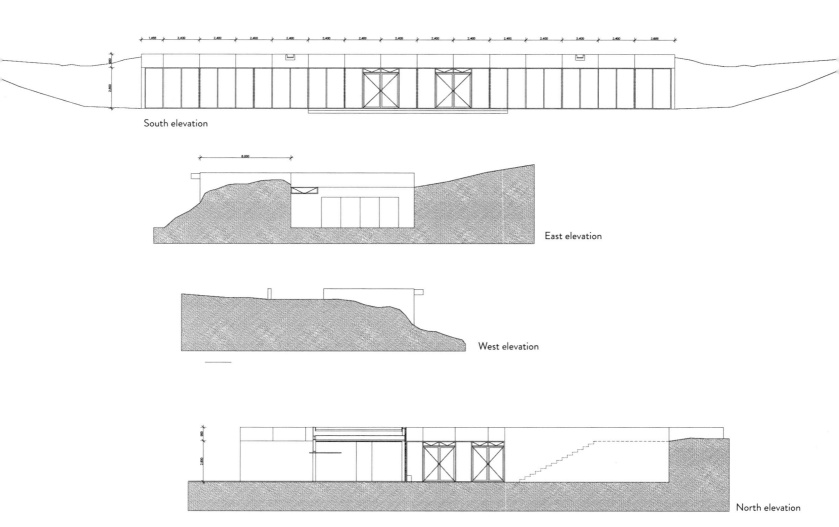

South elevation

East elevation

West elevation

North elevation

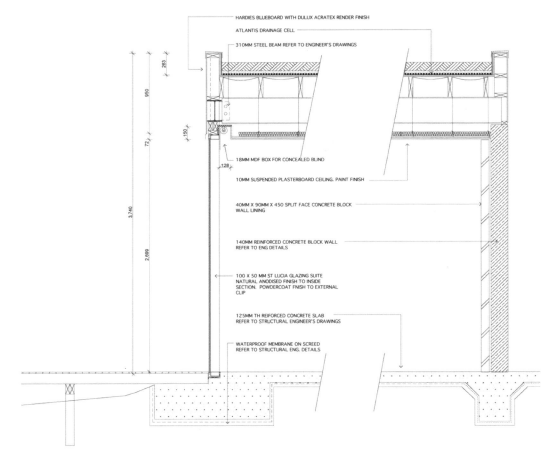

HARDIES BLUEBOARD WITH DULUX ACRATEX RENDER FINISH

ATLANTIS DRAINAGE CELL

310MM STEEL BEAM REFER TO ENGINEER'S DRAWINGS

18MM MDF BOX FOR CONCEALED BLIND

10MM SUSPENDED PLASTERBOARD CEILING. PAINT FINISH

40MM X 90MM X 450 SPLIT FACE CONCRETE BLOCK
WALL LINING

140MM REINFORCED CONCRETE BLOCK WALL
REFER TO ENG DETAILS

100 X 50 MM ST LUCIA GLAZING SUITE
NATURAL ANODISED FINISH TO INSIDE
SECTION. POWDERCOAT FINISH TO EXTERNAL
CLIP

125MM TH REIFORCED CONCRETE SLAB
REFER TO STRUCTURAL ENGINEER'S DRAWINGS

WATERPROOF MEMBRANE ON SCREED
REFER TO STRUCTURAL ENG. DETAILS

Constructive details

Section_A

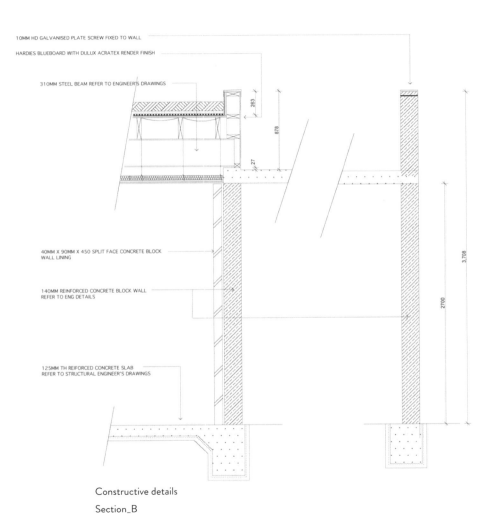

10MM HD GALVANISED PLATE SCREW FIXED TO WALL

HARDIES BLUEBOARD WITH DULUX ACRATEX RENDER FINISH

310MM STEEL BEAM REFER TO ENGINEER'S DRAWINGS

40MM X 90MM X 450 SPLIT FACE CONCRETE BLOCK
WALL LINING

140MM REINFORCED CONCRETE BLOCK WALL
REFER TO ENG DETAILS

125MM TH REIFORCED CONCRETE SLAB
REFER TO STRUCTURAL ENGINEER'S DRAWINGS

263

878

27

3.708

2700

Constructive details

Section_B

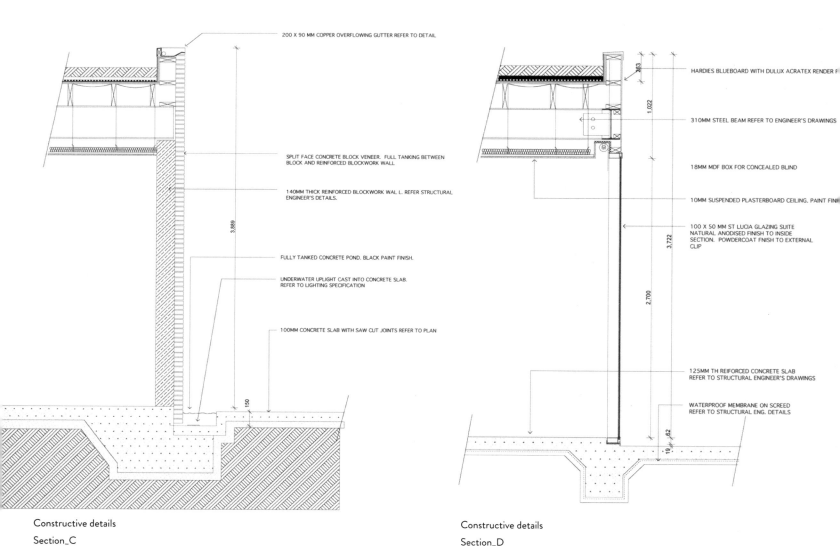

200 X 90 MM COPPER OVERFLOWING GUTTER REFER TO DETAIL

SPLIT FACE CONCRETE BLOCK VENEER. FULL TANKING BETWEEN BLOCK AND REINFORCED BLOCKWORK WALL

140MM THICK REINFORCED BLOCKWORK WAL L. REFER STRUCTURAL ENGINEER'S DETAILS.

FULLY TANKED CONCRETE POND. BLACK PAINT FINISH.

UNDERWATER UPLIGHT CAST INTO CONCRETE SLAB. REFER TO LIGHTING SPECIFICATION

100MM CONCRETE SLAB WITH SAW CUT JOINTS REFER TO PLAN

HARDIES BLUEBOARD WITH DULUX ACRATEX RENDER F

310MM STEEL BEAM REFER TO ENGINEER'S DRAWINGS

18MM MDF BOX FOR CONCEALED BLIND

10MM SUSPENDED PLASTERBOARD CEILING. PAINT FINI

100 X 50 MM ST LUCIA GLAZING SUITE NATURAL ANODISED FINISH TO INSIDE SECTION. POWDERCOAT FNISH TO EXTERNAL CLIP

125MM TH REIFORCED CONCRETE SLAB REFER TO STRUCTURAL ENGINEER'S DRAWINGS

WATERPROOF MEMBRANE ON SCREED REFER TO STRUCTURAL ENG. DETAILS

Constructive details

Section_C

Constructive details

Section_D

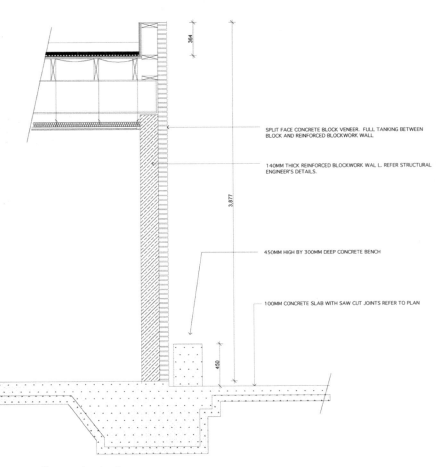

364

3,877

SPLIT FACE CONCRETE BLOCK VENEER. FULL TANKING BETWEEN
BLOCK AND REINFORCED BLOCKWORK WALL

140MM THICK REINFORCED BLOCKWORK WAL L. REFER STRUCTURAL
ENGINEER'S DETAILS.

450MM HIGH BY 300MM DEEP CONCRETE BENCH

100MM CONCRETE SLAB WITH SAW CUT JOINTS REFER TO PLAN

450

Constructive details

Section_E

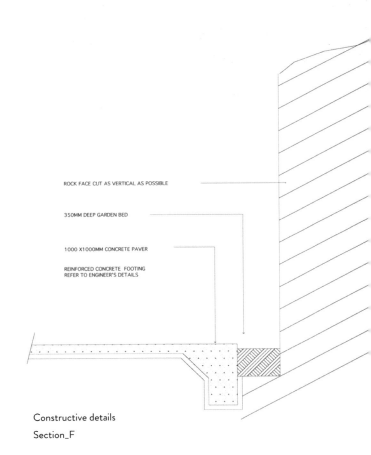

ROCK FACE CUT AS VERTICAL AS POSSIBLE

350MM DEEP GARDEN BED

1000 X1000MM CONCRETE PAVER

REINFORCED CONCRETE FOOTING
REFER TO ENGINEER'S DETAILS

Constructive details

Section_F

Eagle Harbor Cabin

Finne Architects
Lake Superior, MI, USA
Photos © Eric Hausman

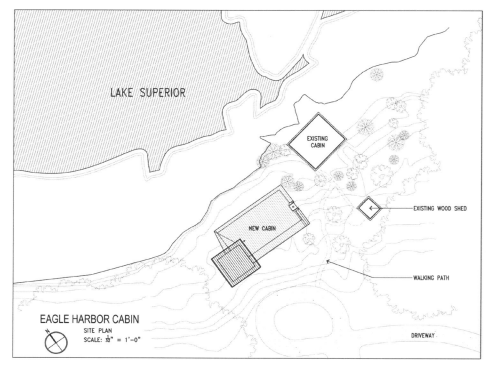

LAKE SUPERIOR

EXISTING CABIN

EXISTING WOOD SHED

NEW CABIN

WALKING PATH

DRIVEWAY

EAGLE HARBOR CABIN
SITE PLAN
SCALE: 1/32" = 1'-0"

Site plan

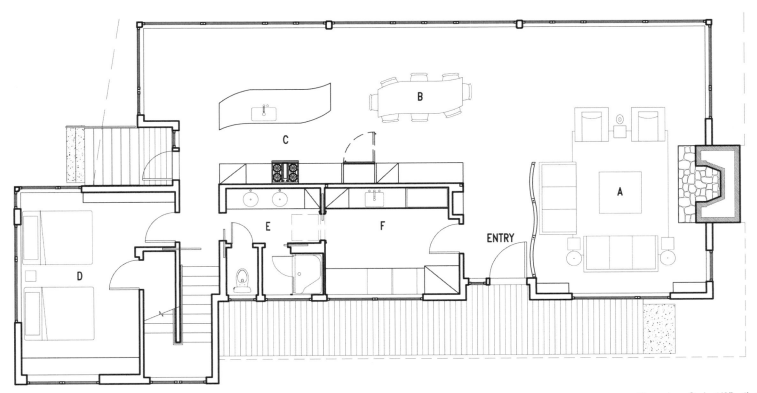

Floor plan - Scale: 1/8" = 1' -0

A. Living area
B. Dining
C. Kitchen
D. Bedroom
E. Bathroom
F. Laundry

Downing Residence

Ibarra Rosano Design Architects
Tucson, AZ, USA
Photos © Bill Timmerman

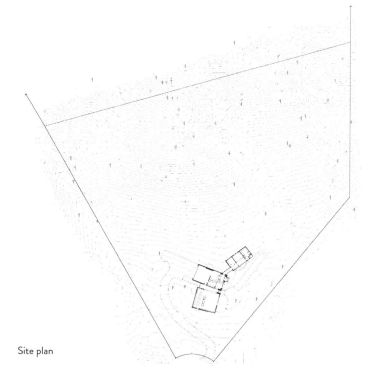

Site plan

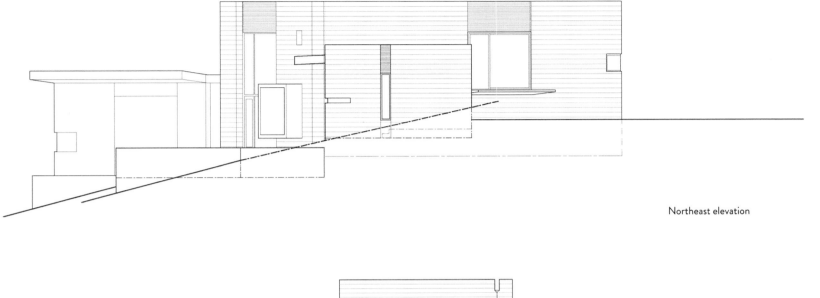

Northeast elevation

Northwest elevation

Southwest elevation

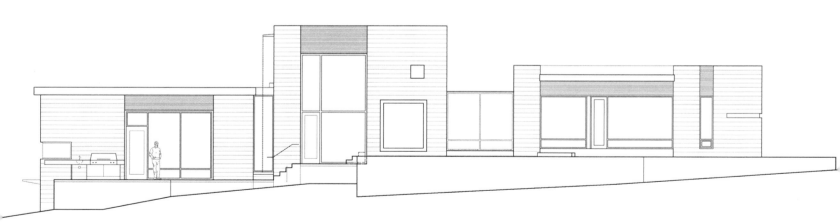

Southeast elevation

Floor plan

HSU House

Epiphyte LAB LLC
Daby, NY, USA
Photos © Jerome & Susan Kaye, Simon Wheeler, Epiphyte Lab LLC

Blue sidings (Hardie boards)
JH 10-20, JH 40-10, JH 40-20

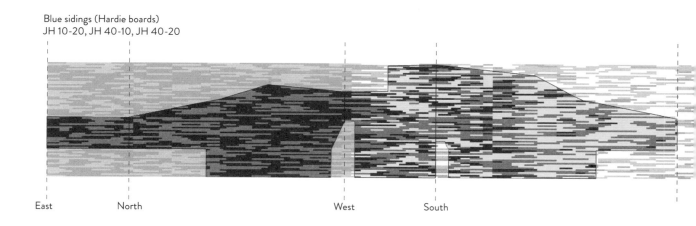

East   North   West   South

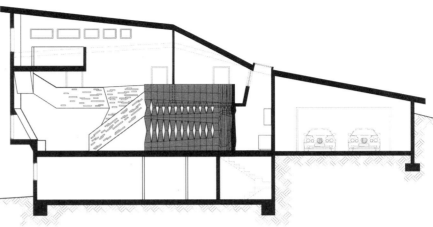

Section

3D plan

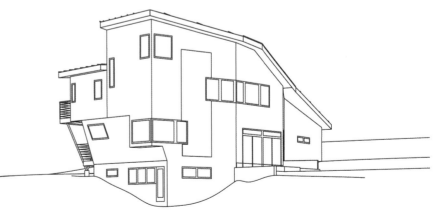

Structure plan

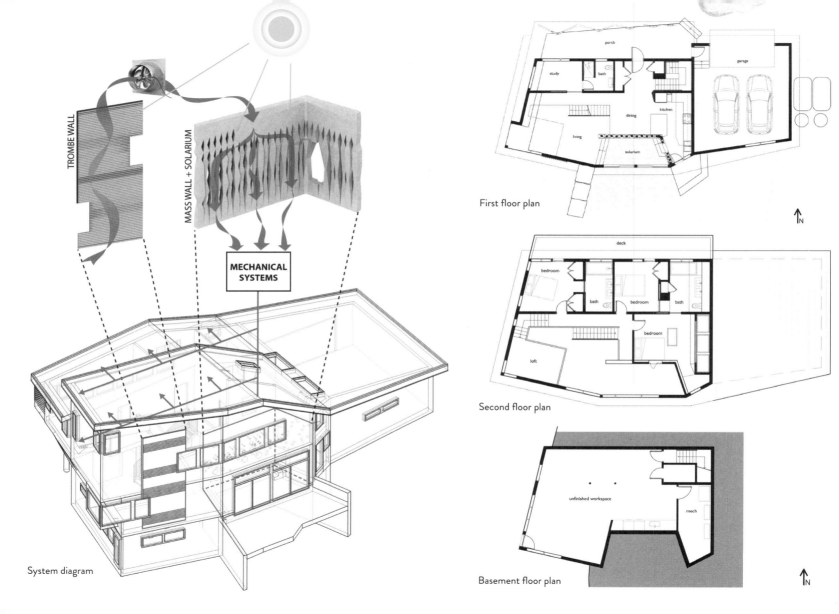

TROMBE WALL

MASS WALL + SOLARIUM

MECHANICAL SYSTEMS

System diagram

First floor plan

porch

study

bath

dining

kitchen

living

solarium

garage

N

Second floor plan

deck

bedroom

bath

bedroom

bath

loft

bedroom

N

Basement floor plan

unfinished workspace

mech

N

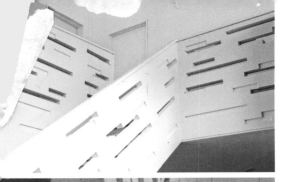

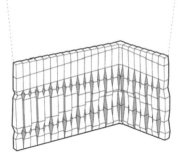

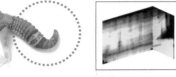

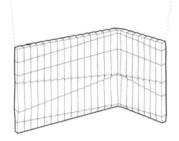

Thickness Variation Based on Insolation Data

Maximize Thermal Properties of Mass Wall

Normal Mass Wall

Thickness Variation

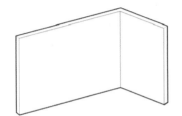

Perforation Variation Based on Insolation Data

Maximize Direct/Indirect Daylight Conditions

Adjustments Based on Program Requirements

Create Viewports + Visual Connections

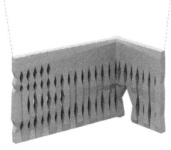

Perforation

Final Adjustments

Poli House

Pezo von Ellrichshausen Architects
Península de Coliumo, Chile
Photos © Cristobal Palma

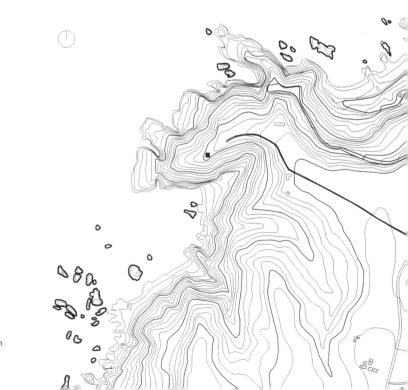

Site plan

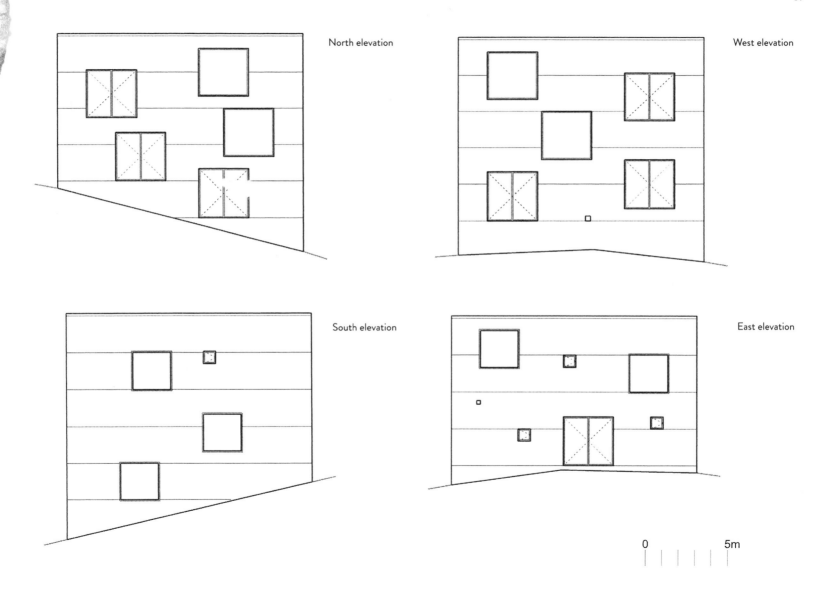

North elevation

West elevation

South elevation

East elevation

0   5m

Ground floor plan

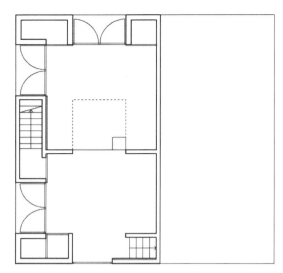

First floor plan

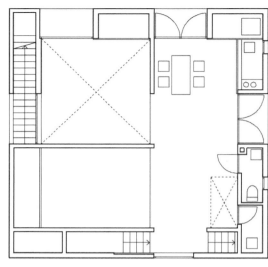

Second floor plan

Roof

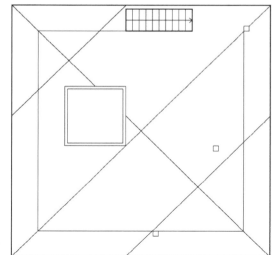

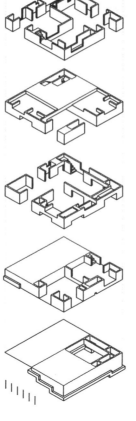

Axonometric view

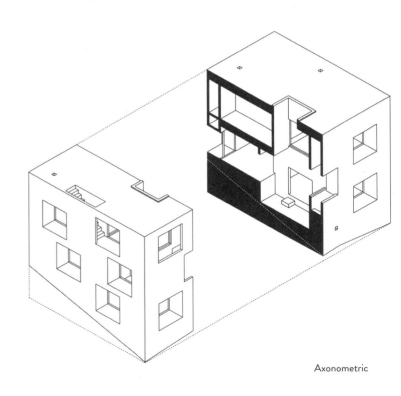

Axonometric

Tóló House

Álvaro Leite Siza Vieira
Lugar Das Carvalhinhas, Alvite, Portugal
Photos © Fernando Guerra

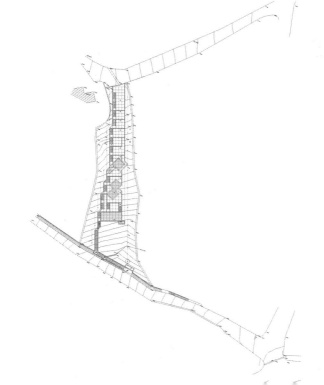

Site plan

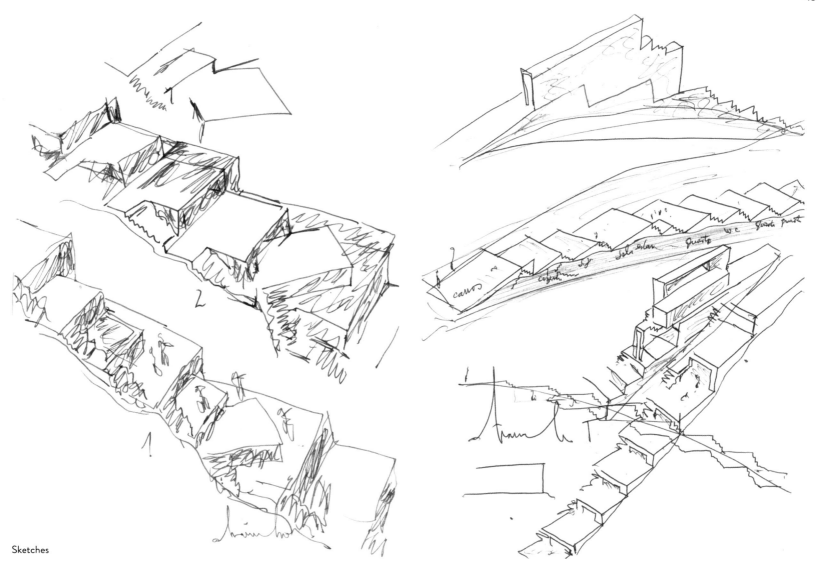

Sketches

East elevation

South elevation

West elevation

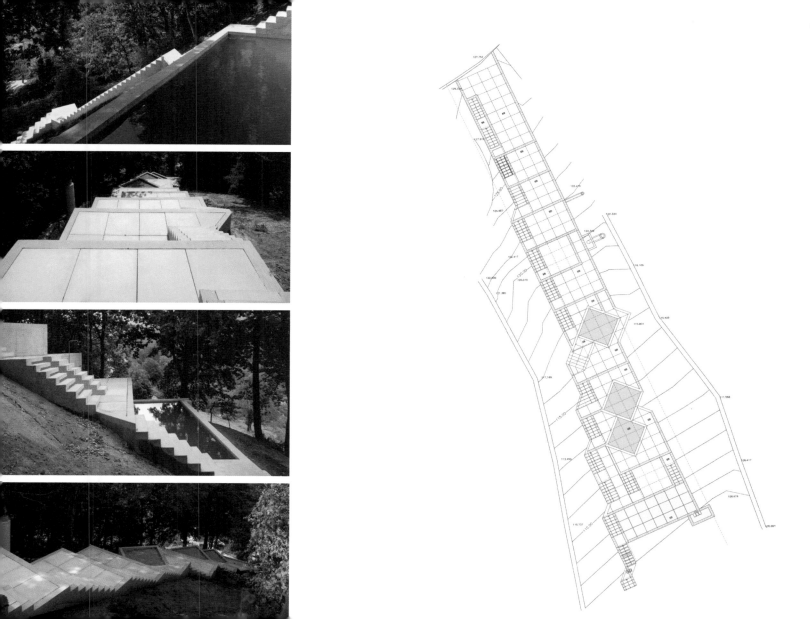

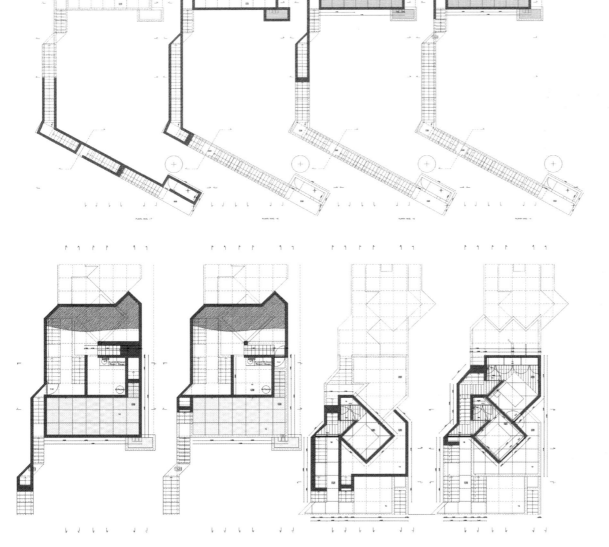

Plants levels 7 to 400

Plants levels 3 to 0

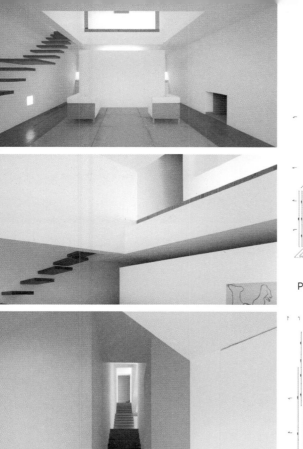

Plants levels 1 to 5

Plants levels 6 to 9

Kyle House

Estes / Twombly Architects
Brewster, MA, USA
Photos © Warren Jagger Photography

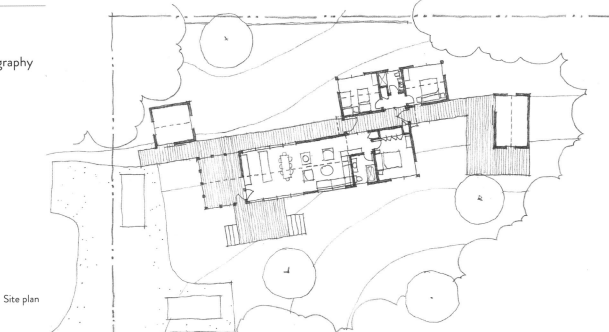

Site plan

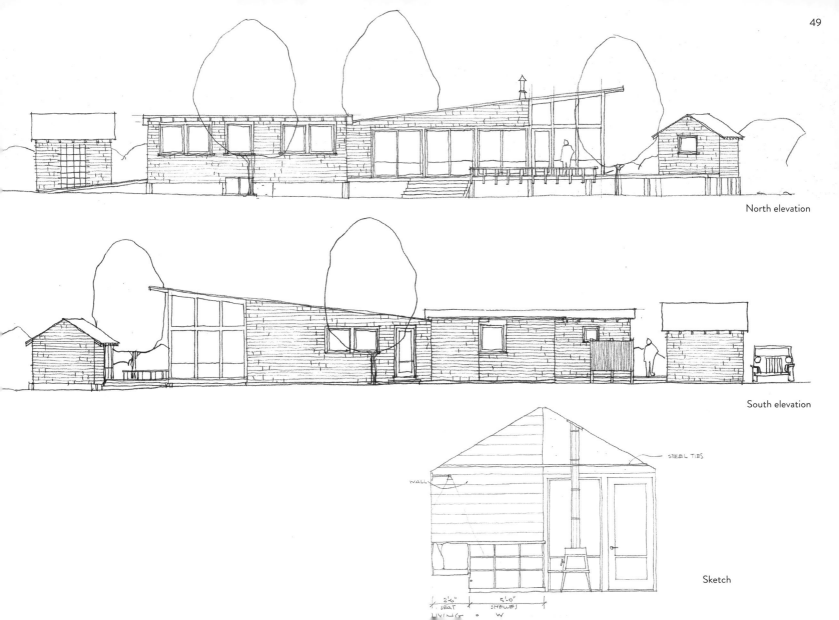

North elevation

South elevation

Sketch

Cliff House

Altius Architecture INC
Muskoka Lakes, Ontario, Canada
Photos © Altius Architecture INC

Site plan

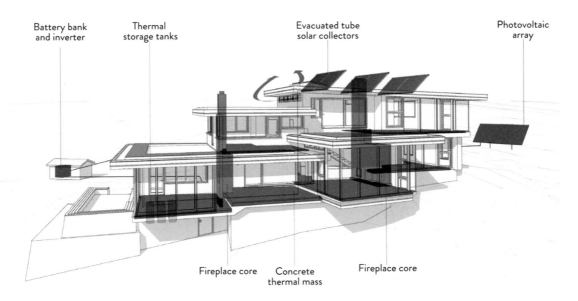

Battery bank and inverter

Thermal storage tanks

Evacuated tube solar collectors

Photovoltaic array

Fireplace core

Concrete thermal mass

Fireplace core

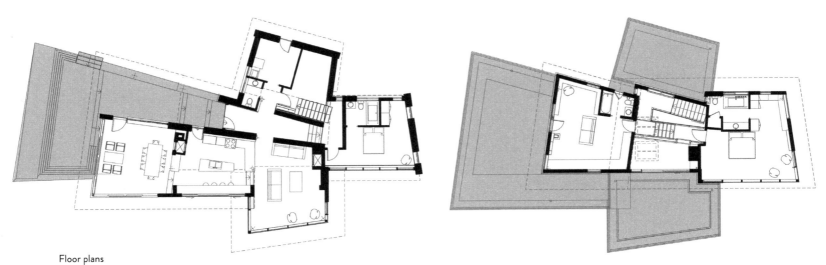

Floor plans

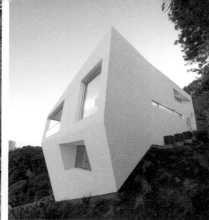

Hill House

Johnston Marklee & Associates
Pacific Palisades, CA, USA
Photos © Eric Staudenmaier

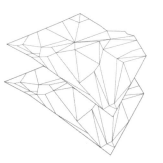
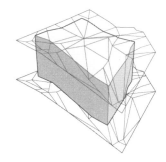
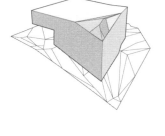

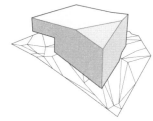
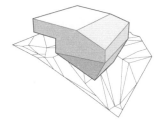

Axonometry sequence

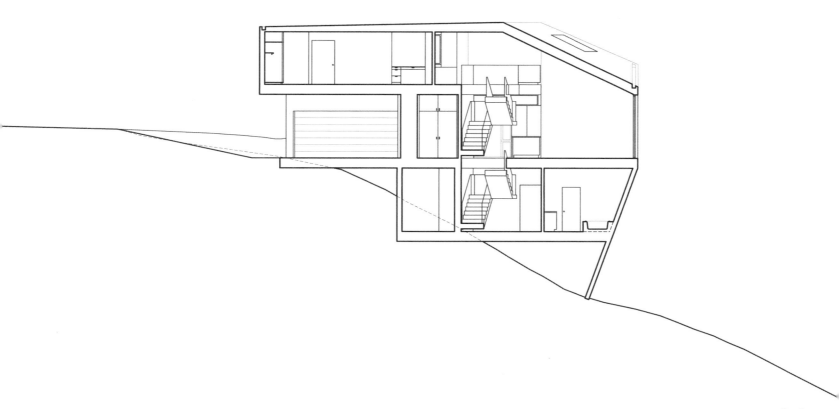

Section

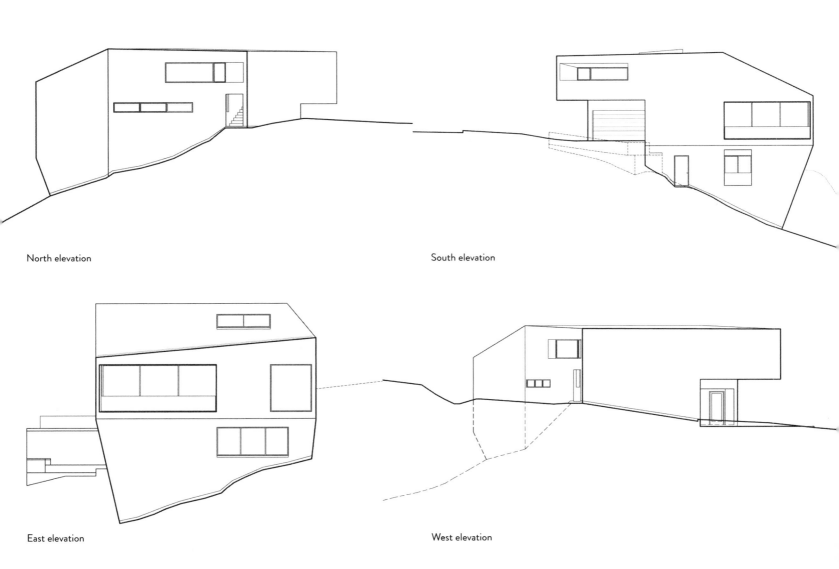

North elevation

South elevation

East elevation

West elevation

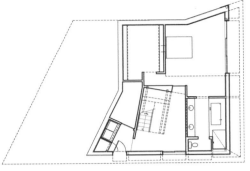

First floor plan

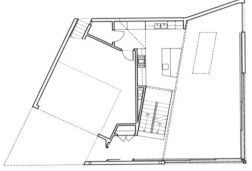

Second floor plan

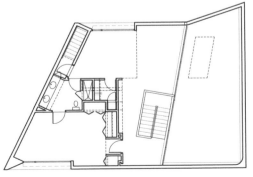

Third floor plan

House in Rigi Scheidegg

Andreas Fuhrimann Gabrielle Hächler Architekten
Rigi Scheidegg, Switzerland
Photos © Valentin Jeck

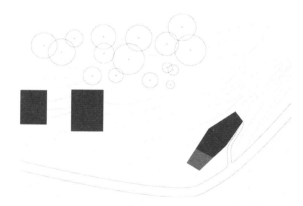

Site plan

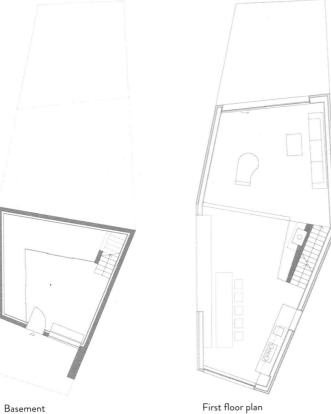

Basement

First floor plan

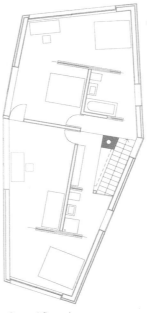

Second floor plan

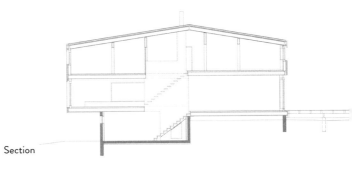

Section

O-S House

Johnsen Schmaling Architects
Racine, WI, USA
Photos © Johnsen Schmaling Architects

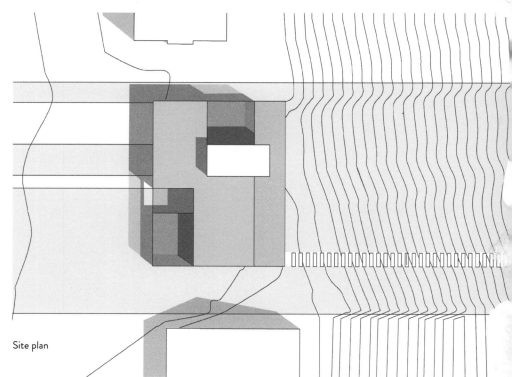

Site plan

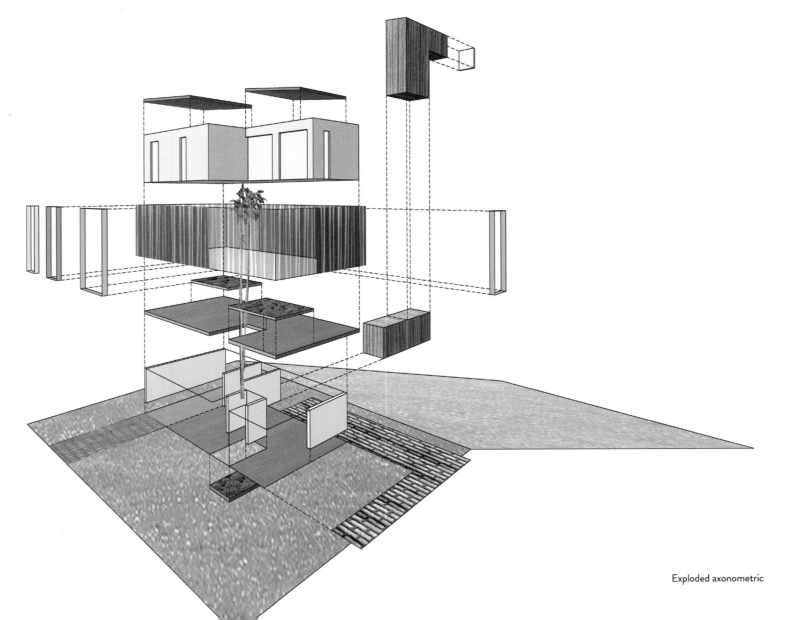

Exploded axonometric

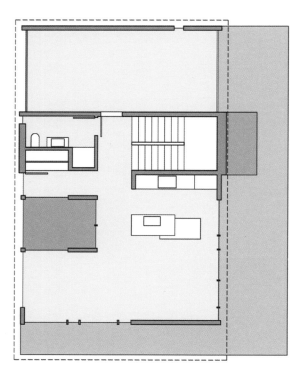
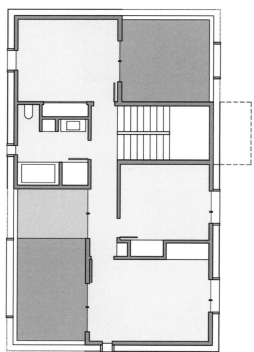
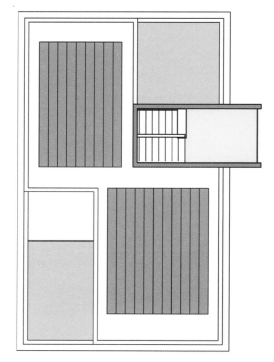

Floor plans

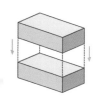

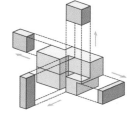

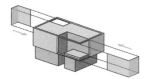
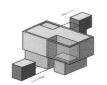

Morphology

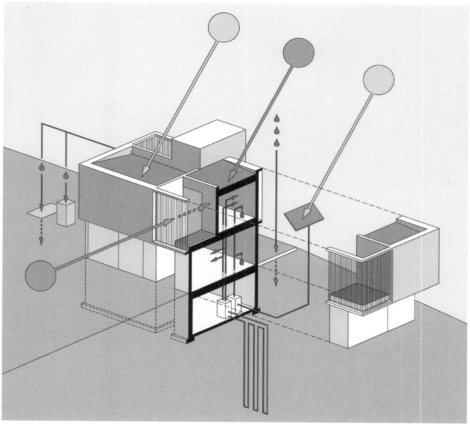

Sustainability diagram

Villa in Katsuura

Chiba Manabu/Chiba Manabu Architects
Katsuura-Shi, Chiba, Japan
Photos © Nácasa & Partners

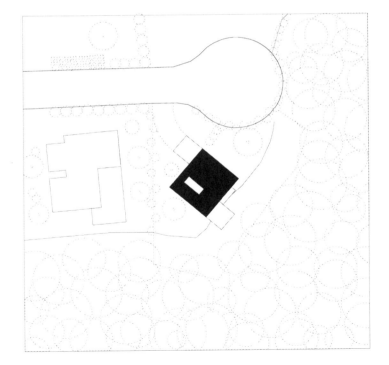

Site plan

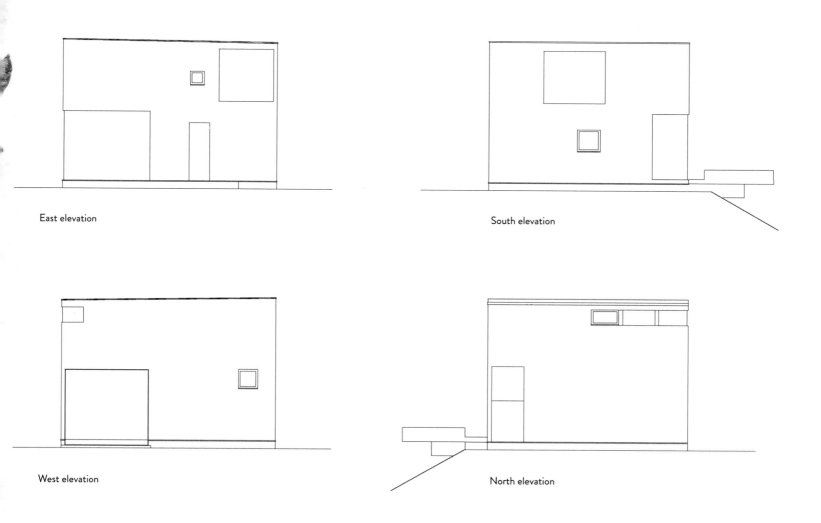

East elevation

South elevation

West elevation

North elevation

63

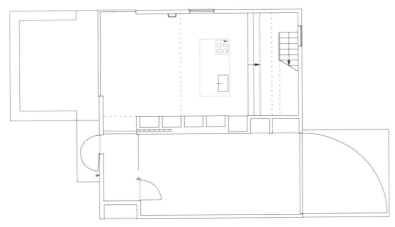

Ground floor plan

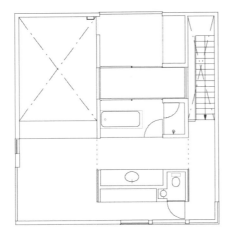

First floor plan

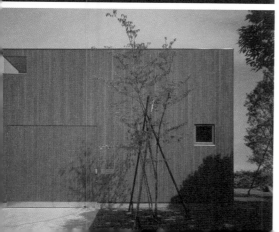

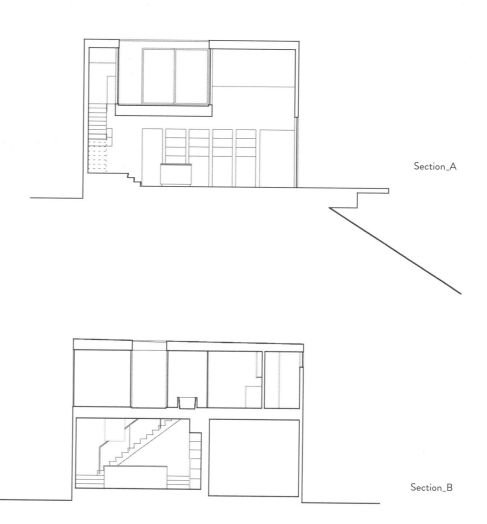

Section_A

Section_B

Garcia Residence

Chiba Ibarra Rosano Design Architects
Tucson, AZ, USA
Photos © Bill Timmerman

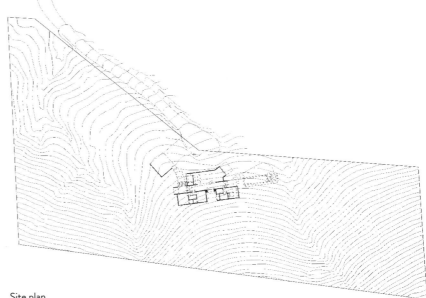

Site plan

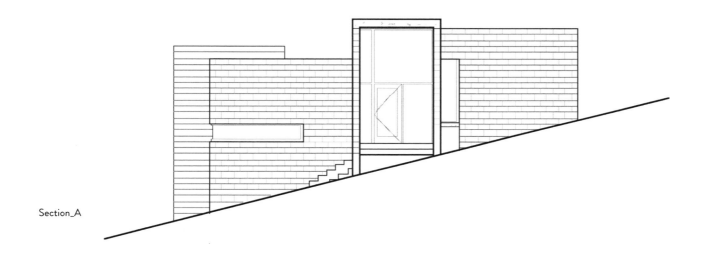

Section_A

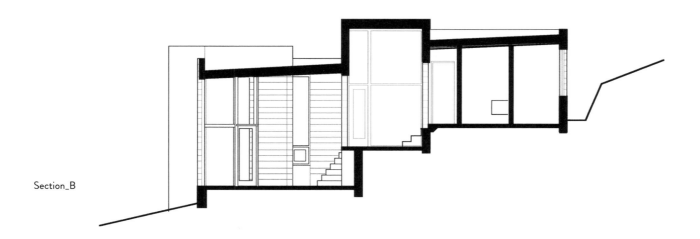

Section_B

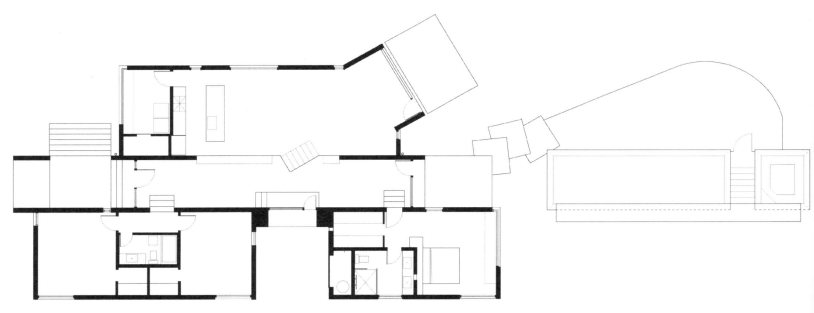

Floor plan

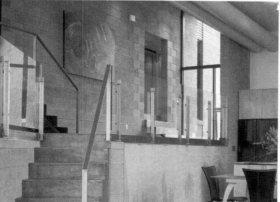

Sketch

Locarno House

Designyougo - Architects and Designers
Solduno, Locarno, Switzerland
Photos © Hiroyuki Oki

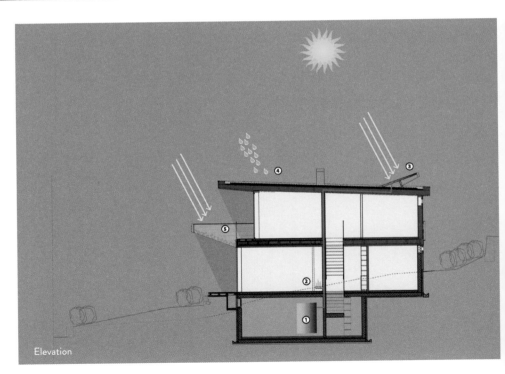

Elevation

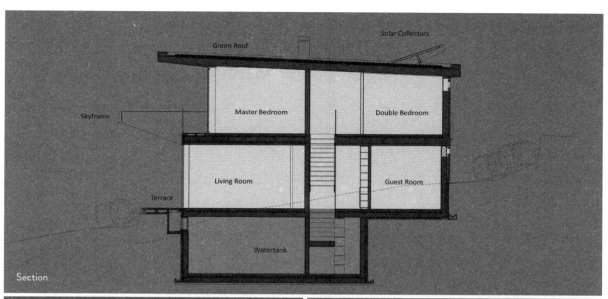

Solar Collectors

Green Roof

Skyframe

Master Bedroom

Double Bedroom

Living Room

Guest Room

Terrace

Watertank

Section

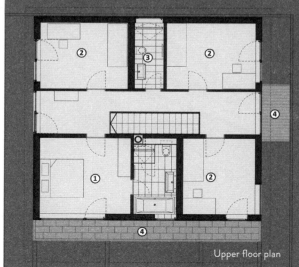

Upper floor plan

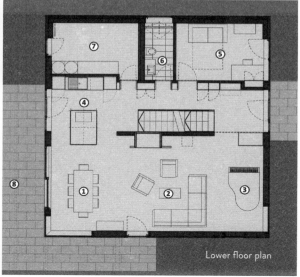

Lower floor plan

Mountain House in Hemsedal

Div.A Arkitekter
Hemsedal, Norway
Photos © Div.A Arkitekter, Michael Perlmutter

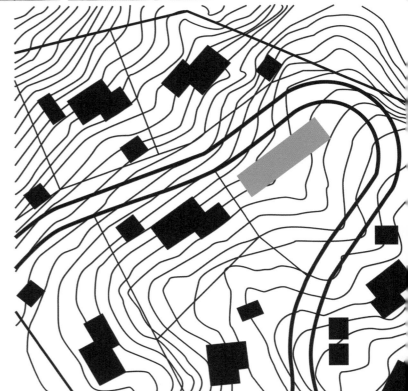

Site plan

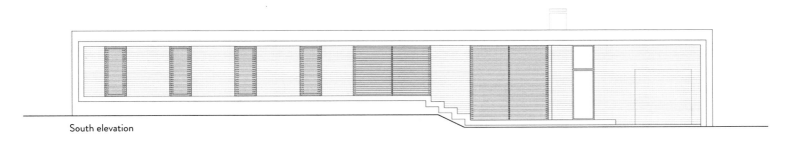

South elevation

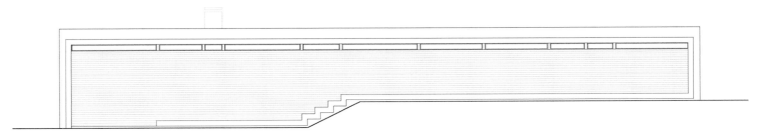

North elevation

East elevation

West elevation

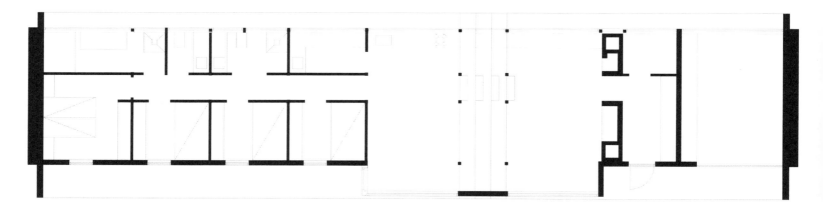

Plant

0   1   5 m

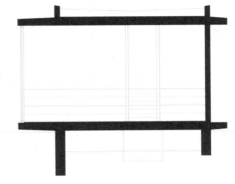

Section A_A

Section B_B

0   1   5 m

TY Pren Eco-House

Feilden Fowles
Trallong, Wales, UK
Photos © David Grandorge, Fergus Feilden

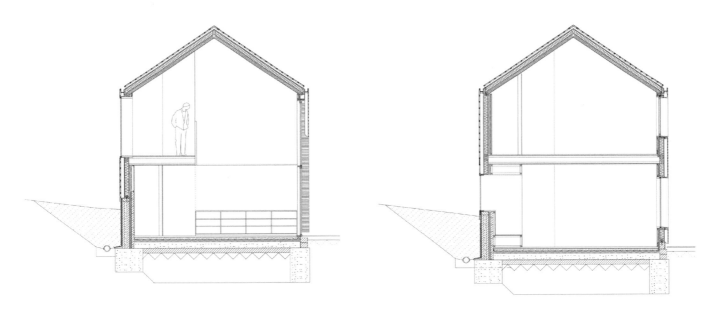

Cross sections

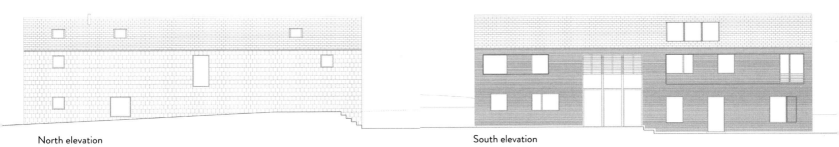

North elevation

South elevation

XSMC House

Estudi d'Arquitectura Set
Port de la Selva, Girona, Spain
Photos © Hiroyuki Oki

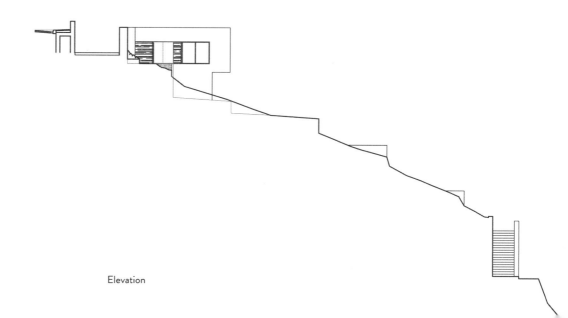

Elevation

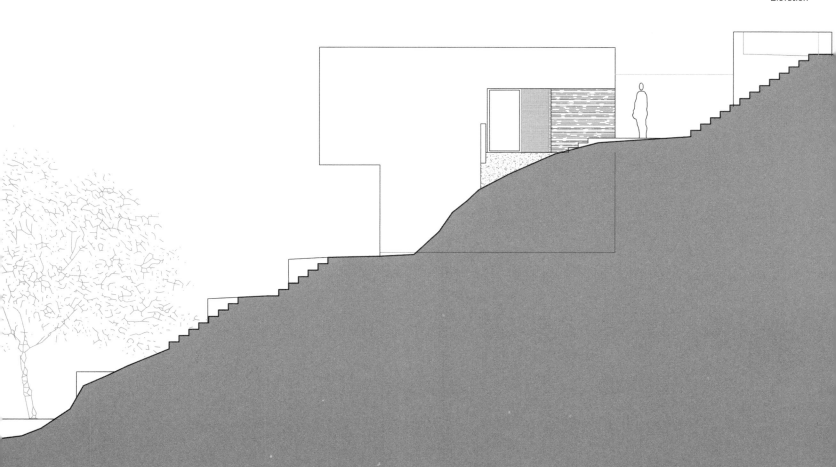

Elevation

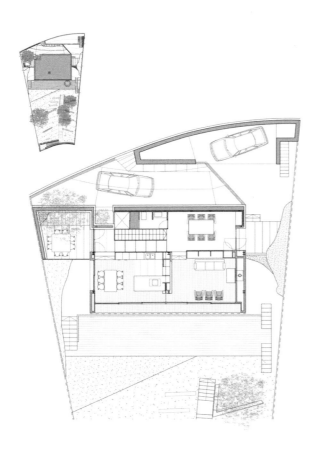

Upper floor plan - Roof plan

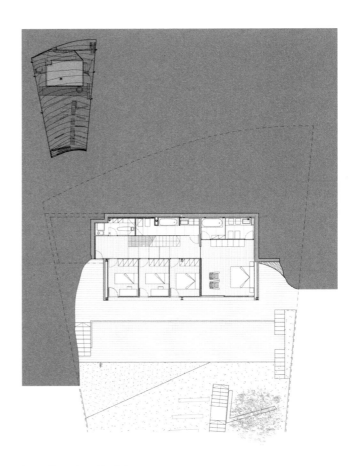

Lower floor plan - Roof plan

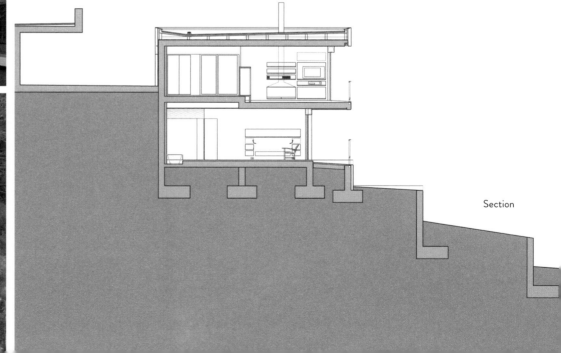

Section

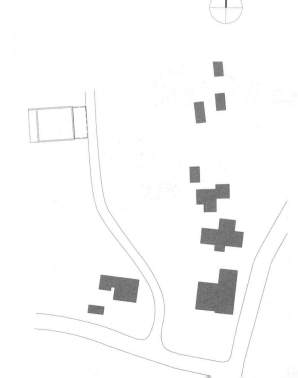

Schmuck House

Hans Gangoly
Graz, Austria
Photos © Paul Ott

Site plan

Basement plan

Upper floor plan

Ceiling plan

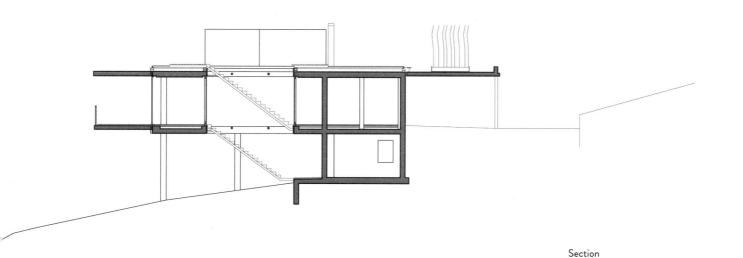

Section

Agosta House

Patkau Architects
San Juan Island, WA, USA
Photos © James Dow / Patkau Architects

Site plan

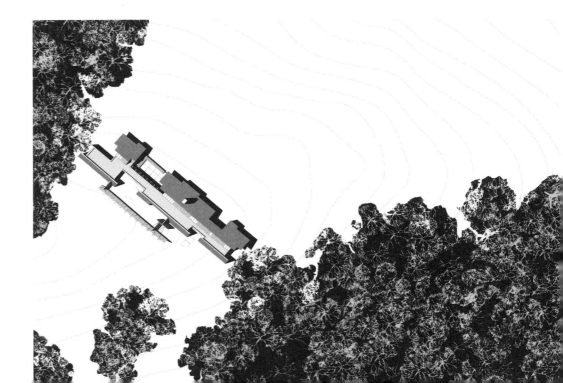

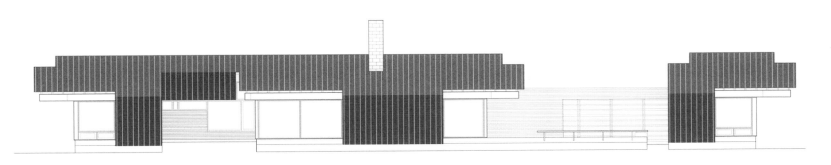

Northeast elevation

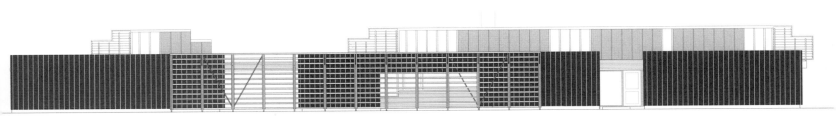

Southeast elevation

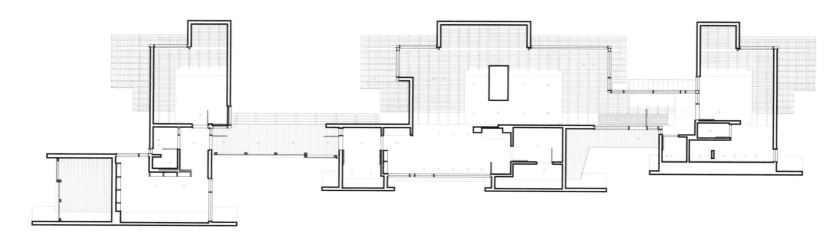

Reflected ceiling plan

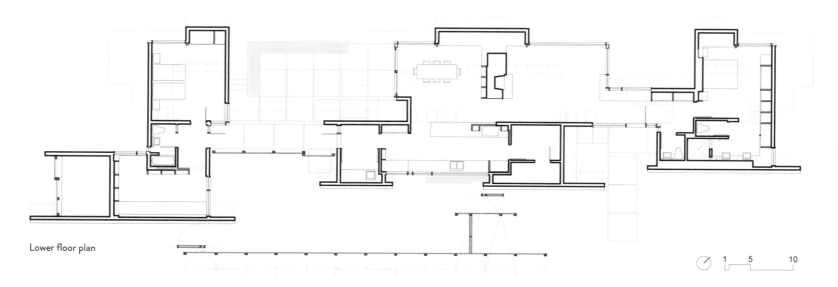

Lower floor plan

1 5 10

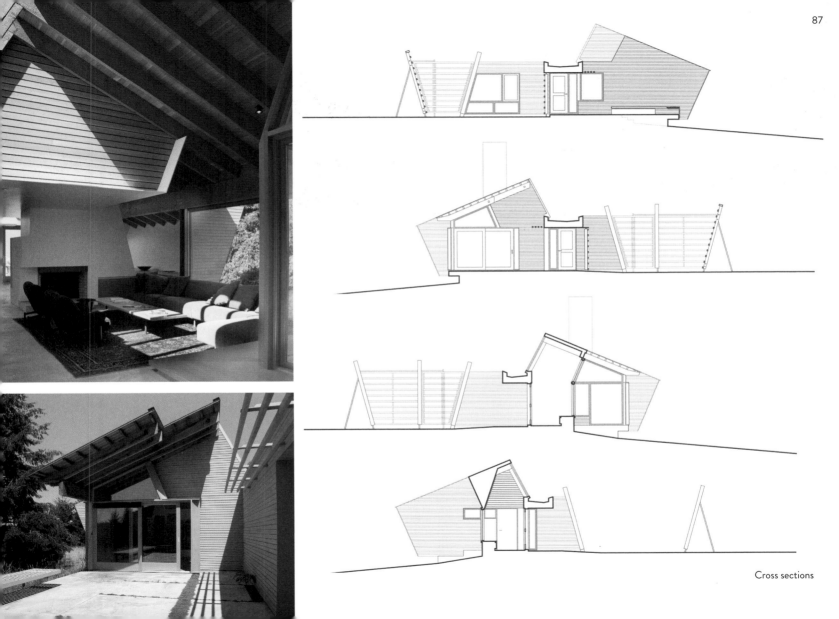

Cross sections

Glass House

Unit Arkitektur AB
Träslövläge, Sweden
Photos © Krister Engström, Unit Arkitektur

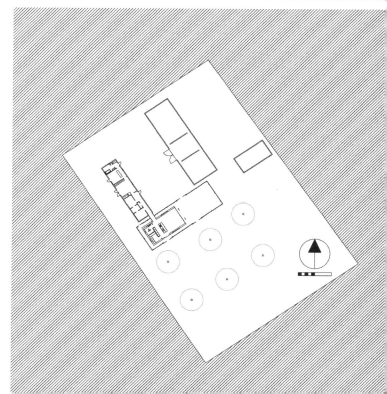

Site plan

89

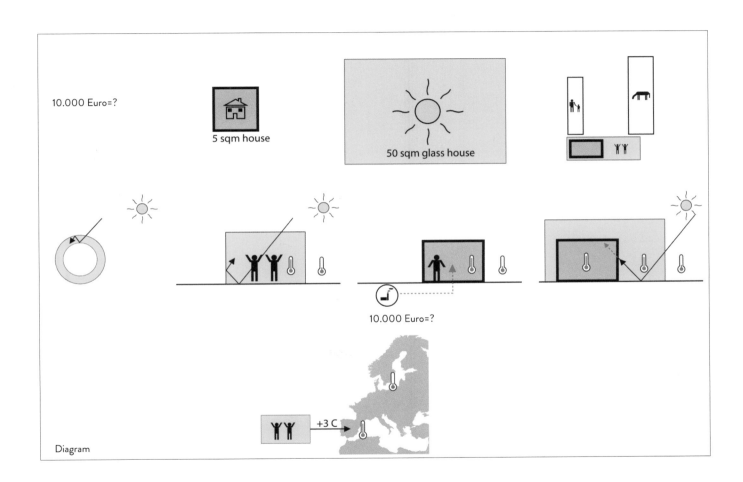

10.000 Euro=?

5 sqm house

50 sqm glass house

10.000 Euro=?

+3 C

Diagram

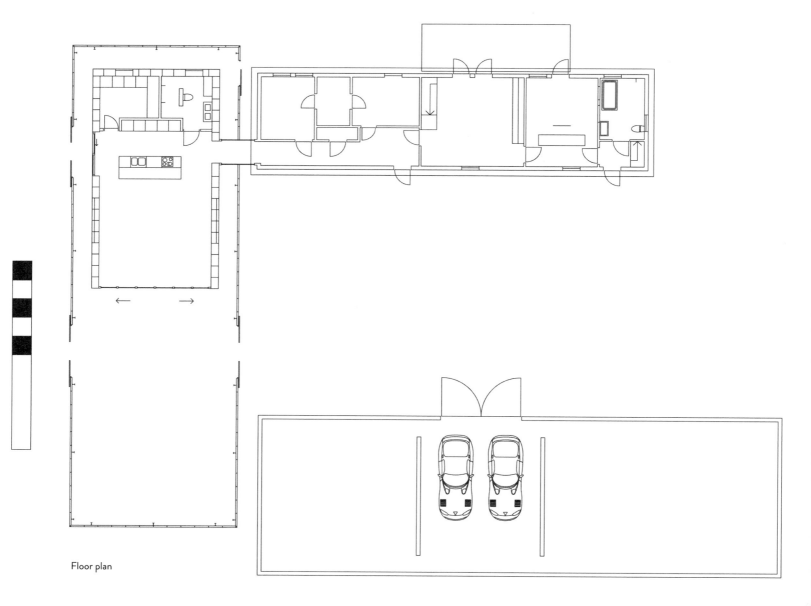

Floor plan

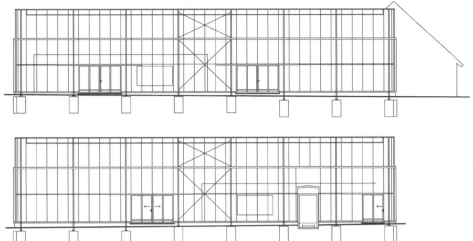

Facades

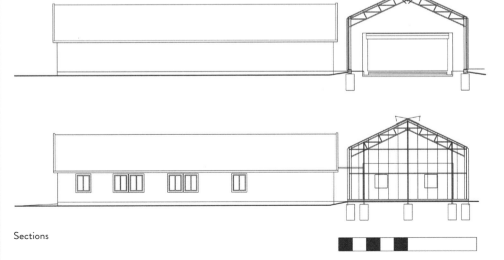

Sections

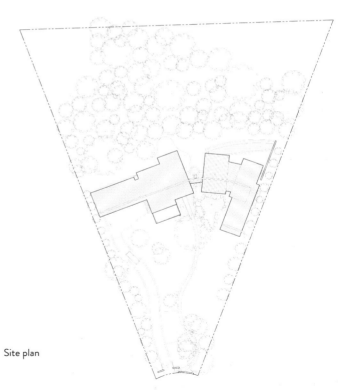

Residence 104

Miró Rivera
Austin, Texas, USA
Photos © Paul Bardagjy

Site plan

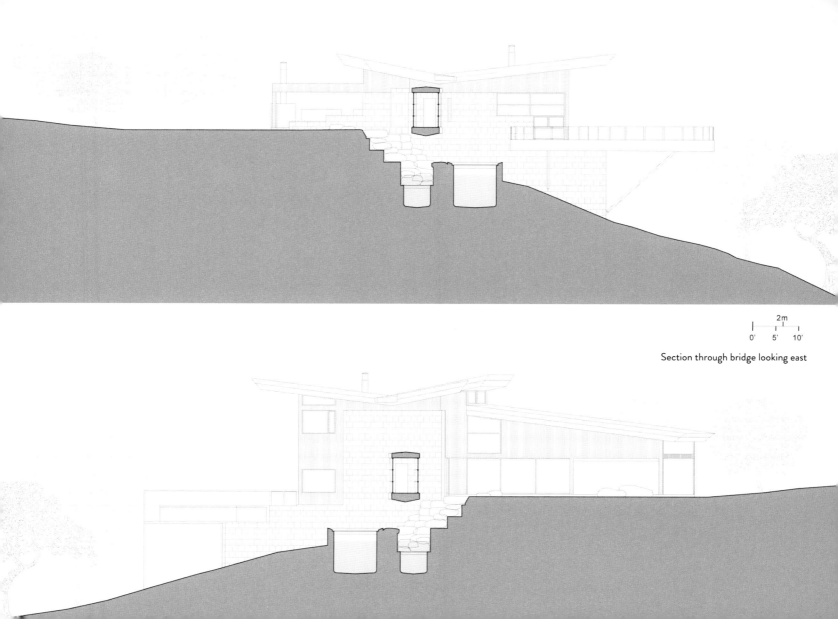

Section through bridge looking east

2m

0'   5'   10'

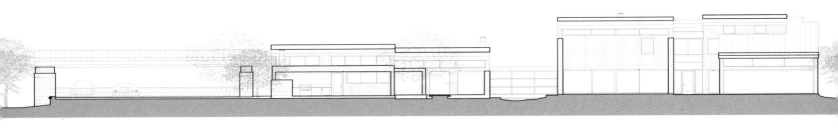

2m
0' 5' 10'

South elevation

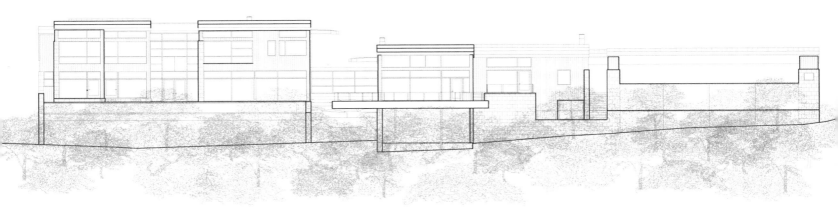

2m
0' 5' 10'

North elevation

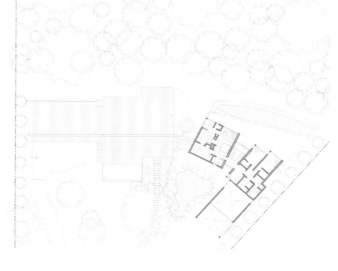

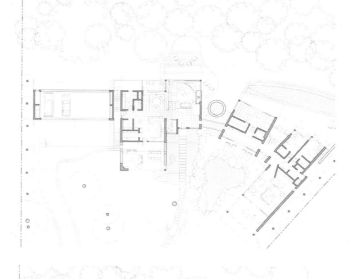

Lower floor plan

Upper floor plan

Brickell Pollock House

Hopkinson Team Architecture
Bethells Beach, New Zealand
Photos © Simon Devitt

Site plan

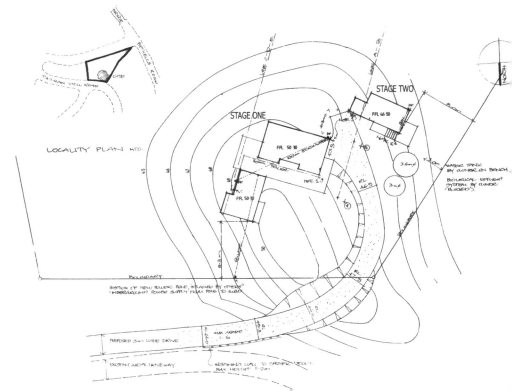

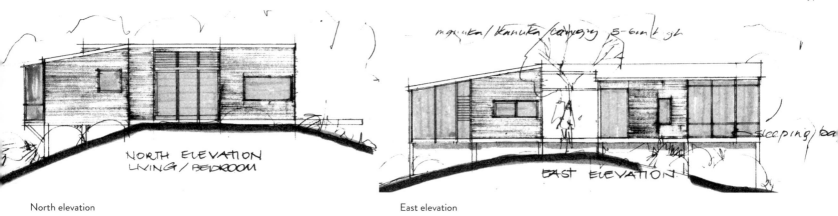

NORTH ELEVATION
LIVING / BEDROOM

North elevation

manuka / kanuka canopy 5-6m high

sleeping / ba

EAST ELEVATION

East elevation

manuka canopy 5-6m high

view to hills

winta sun

BEDROOM

decking

800

glazed bay

sand dunes

ventilators

cantilever floor

SECTION THRU BEDROOM
1:50

North elevation studio

Section

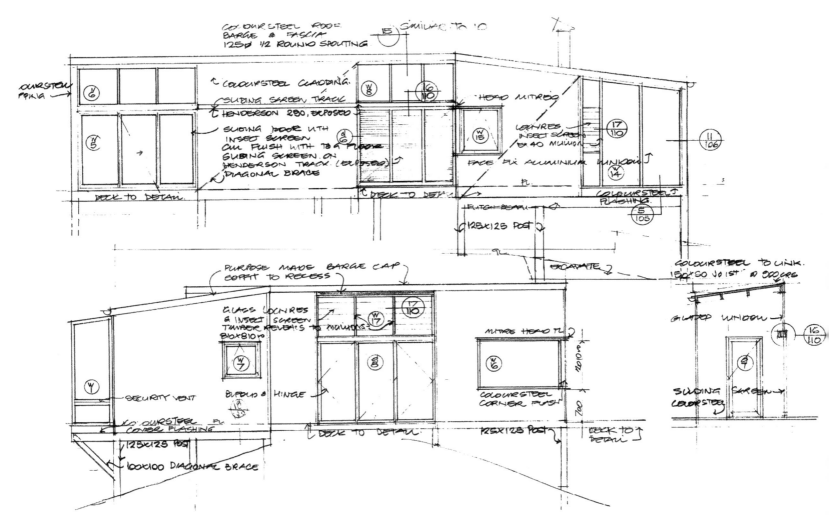

Details

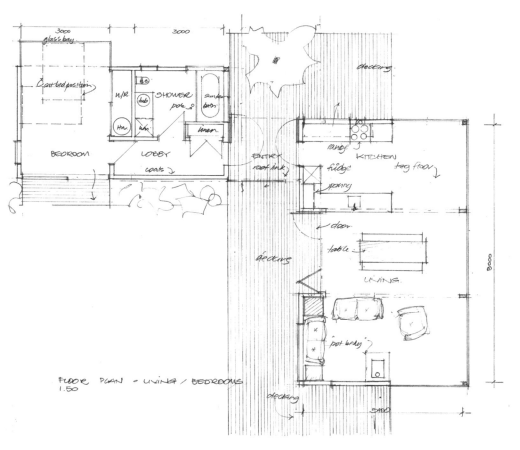

FLOOR PLAN = LIVING / BEDROOMS
1:50

Floor plan

Os House

Nolaster
Loredo, Cantabria, Spain
Photos © José Hevia

Site plan

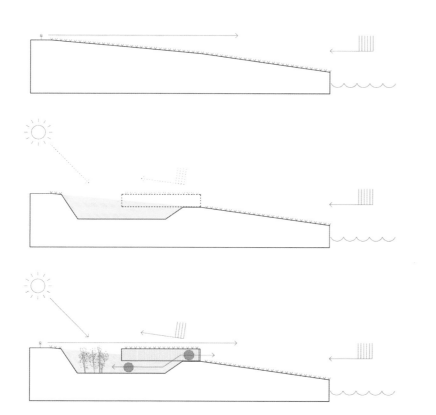

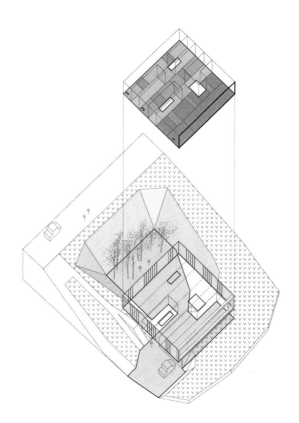

Conceptual scheme

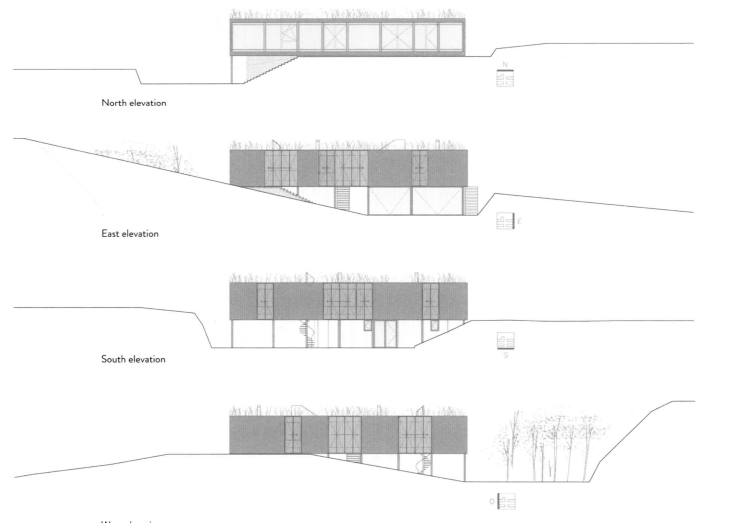

North elevation

East elevation

South elevation

West elevation

ALZADOS

0   1   2   5   10

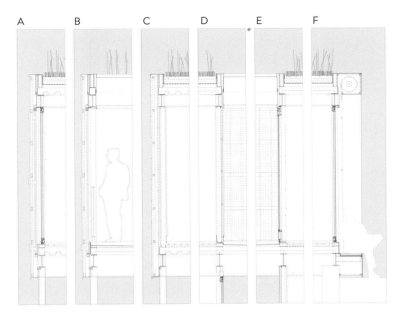

A. Zinc exterior shutters
B. Zinc exterior shutters in patio
C. Zinc facade
D. Enclosures
E. Gap
F. North facade

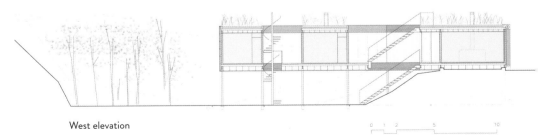

West elevation

0 1 2   5   10

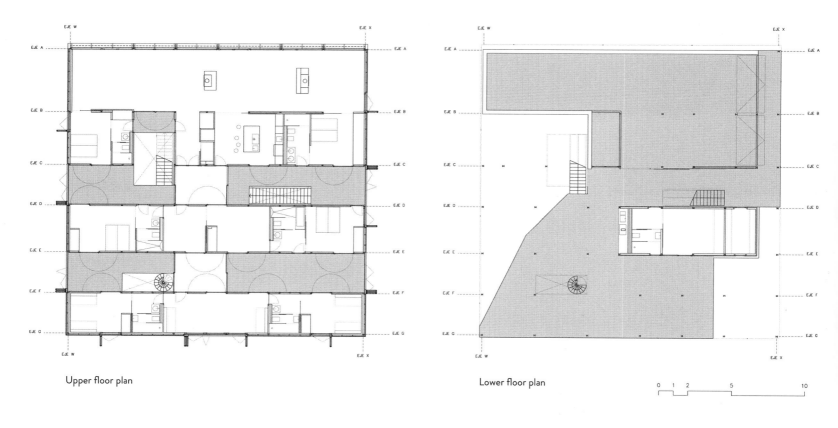

Upper floor plan

Lower floor plan

0 1 2   5   10

Lavaflow 2

Graig Steely
Hawaii, USA
Photos © JD Peterson

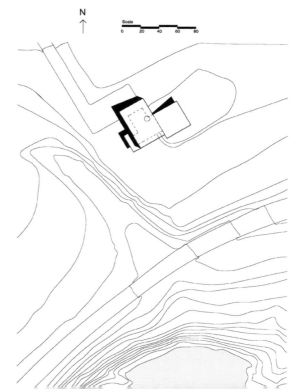

N

Scale
0   20   40   60   80

Site plan

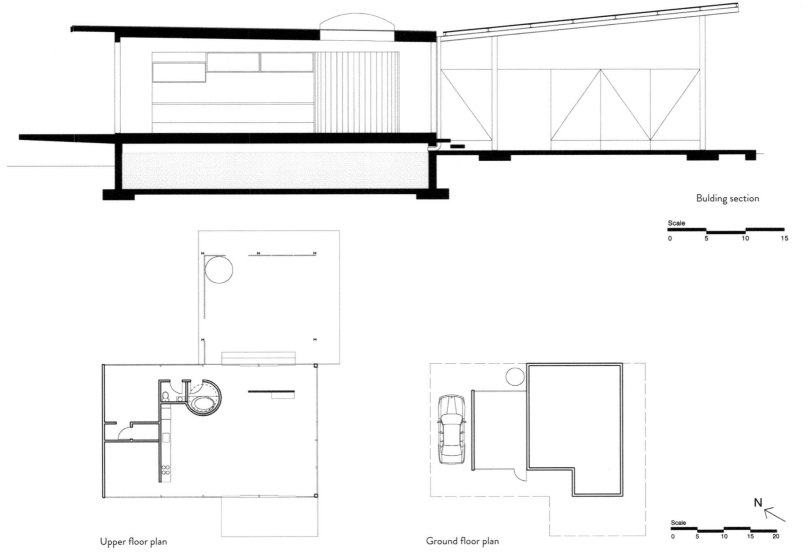

Bulding section

Scale
0   5   10   15

Upper floor plan

Ground floor plan

N

Scale
0   5   10   15   20

House in the Sierra de Arrábida

Eduardo Souto de Moura
Sierra de Arrábida, Portugal
Photos © Luís Ferreira Alves

Site plan

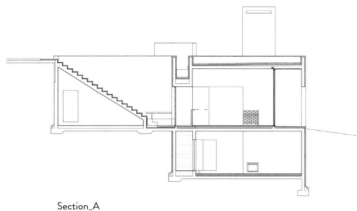

Section_A

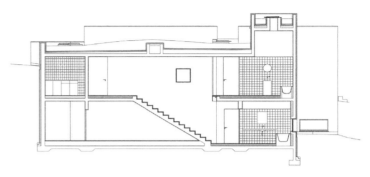

Section_B

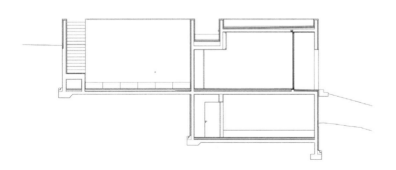

Section_C

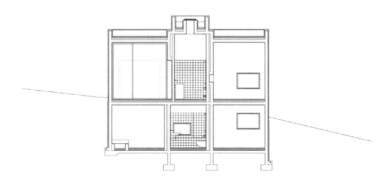

Section_D

0 1 2

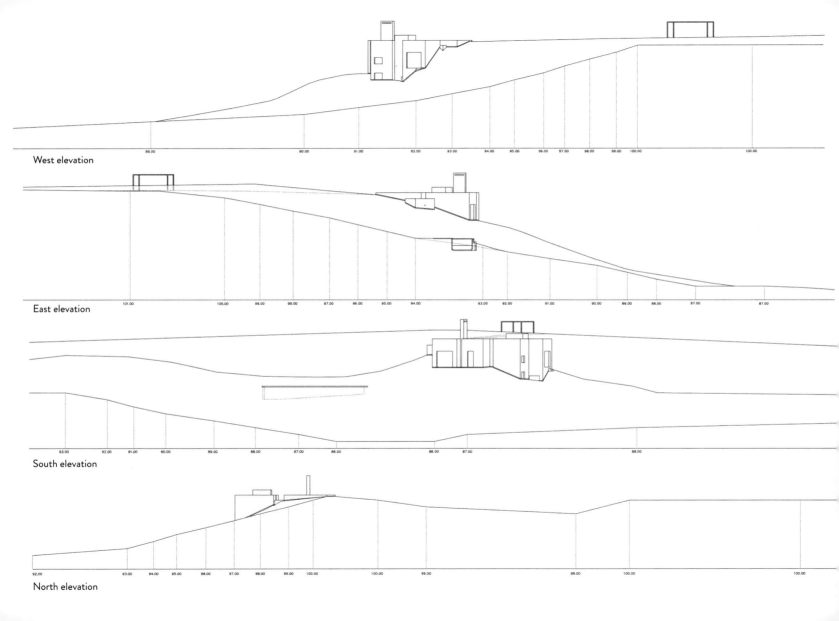

West elevation

East elevation

South elevation

North elevation

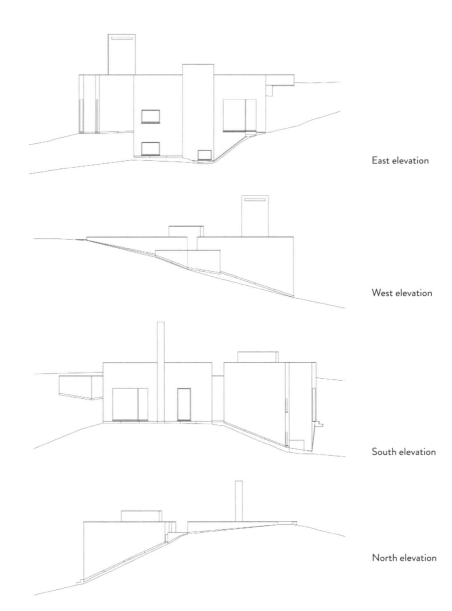

East elevation

West elevation

South elevation

North elevation

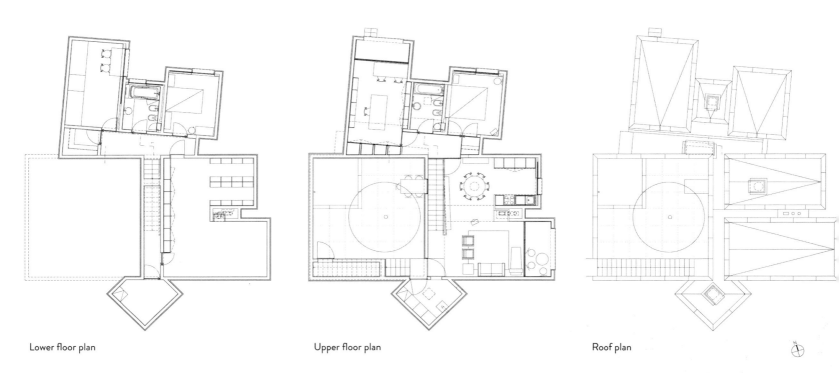

Lower floor plan

Upper floor plan

Roof plan

N

0 1 2

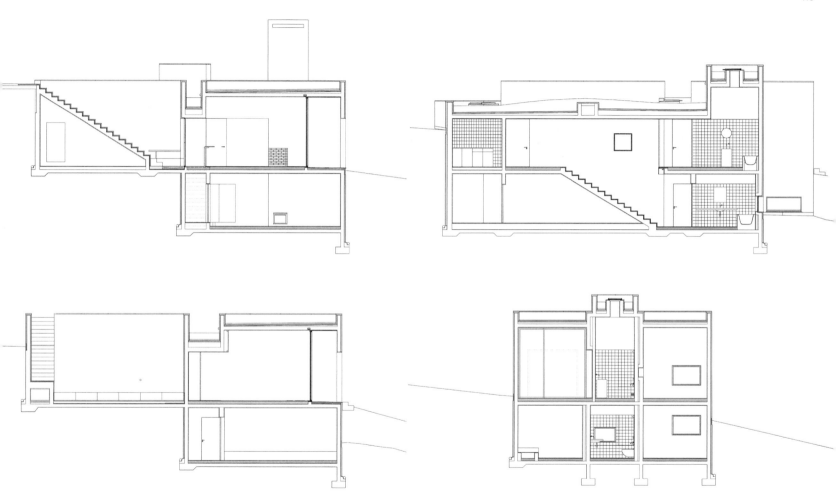

House sections

House in Malibu

Kanner Architects
Malibu, CA, USA
Photos © John Linden

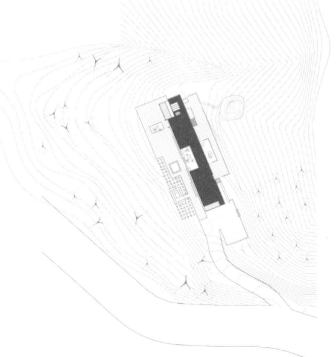

Site plan

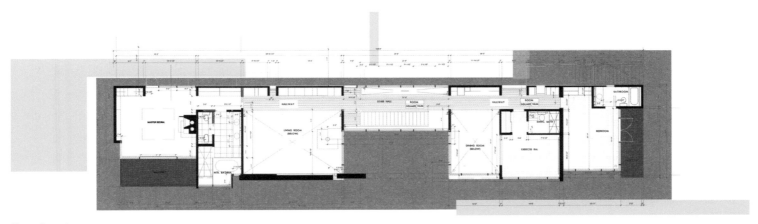

Upper floor plan

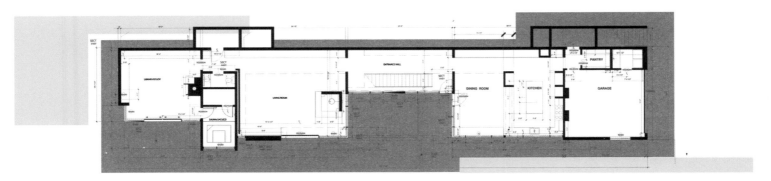

Lower floor plan

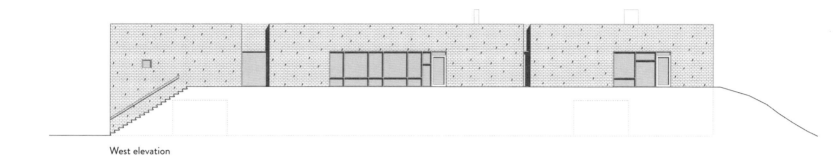

West elevation

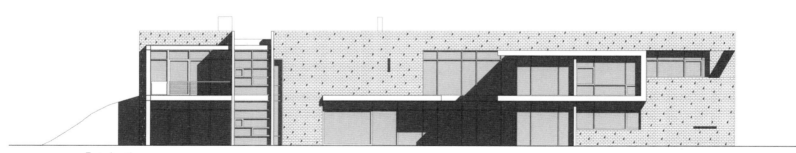

East elevation

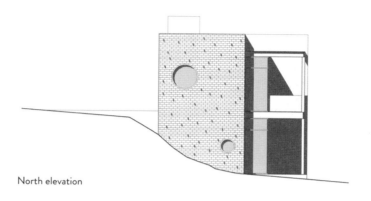

North elevation

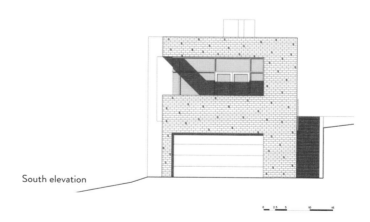

South elevation

0   2.5   5   10   15

House in Vallvidrera

Francisco de la Guardia
Vallvidrera, Spain
Photos © Jordi Miralles

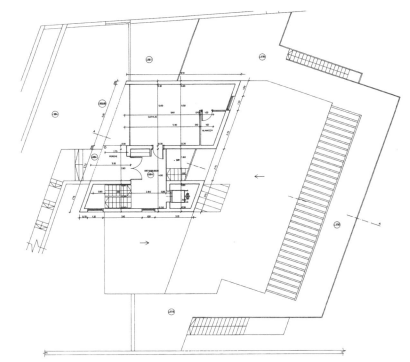

Garage access

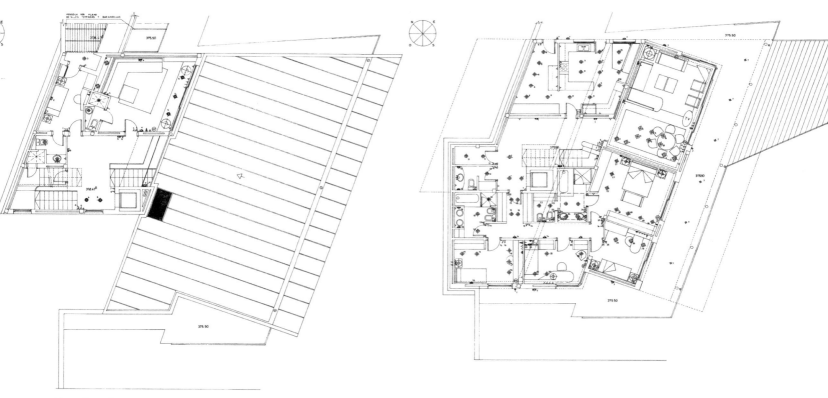

Upper floor plan

Lower floor plan

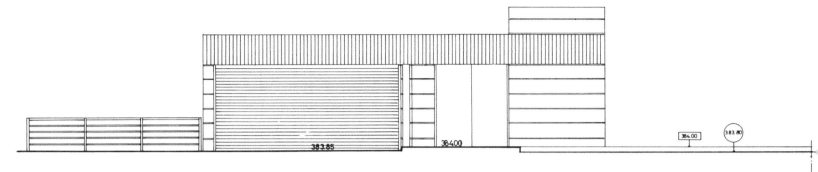

North elevation

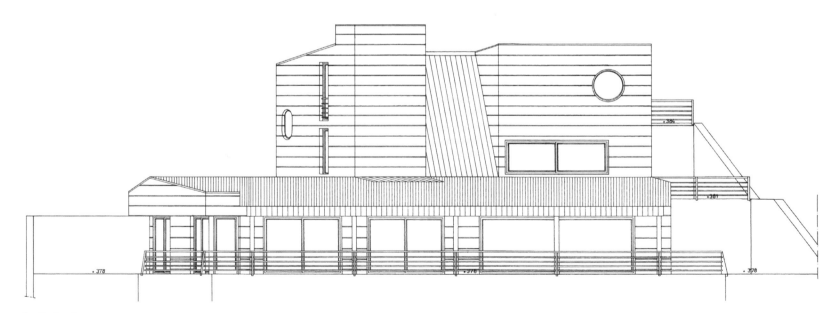

South elevation

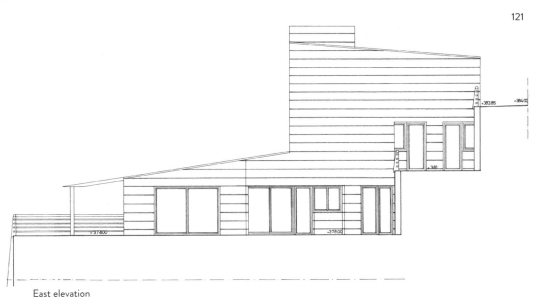

East elevation

West elevation

Rooftecture S

Shuhei Endo Architect Institute
Hyōgo Prefecture, Japan
Photos © Yoshiharu Matsumura

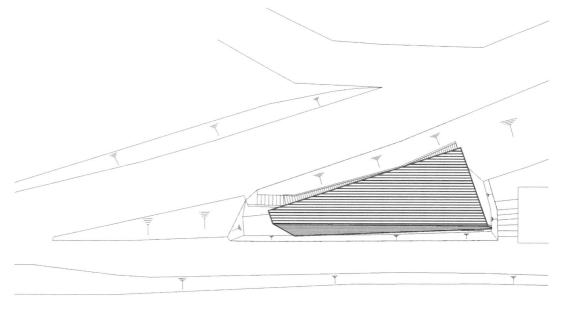

Site plan

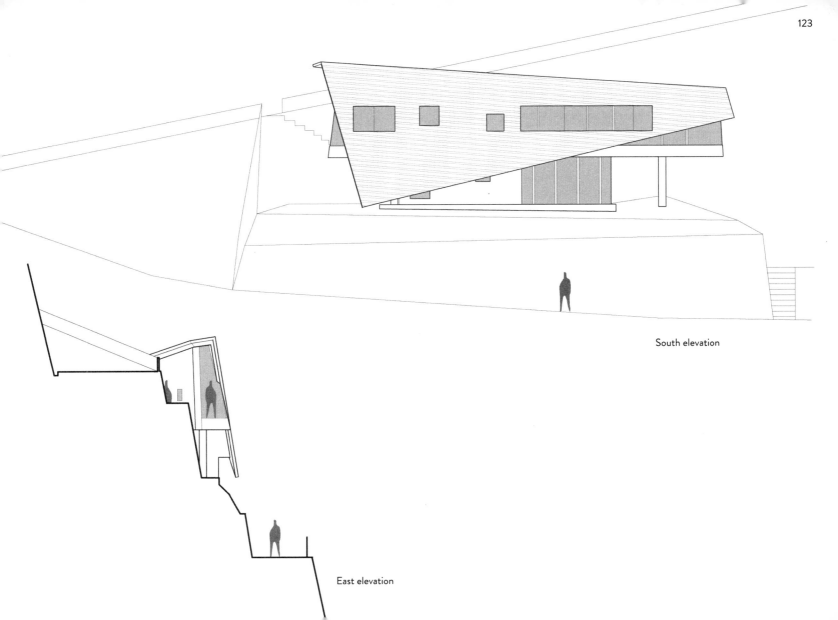

South elevation

East elevation

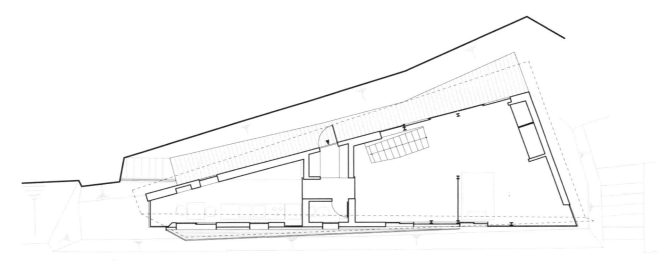

Upper floor plan

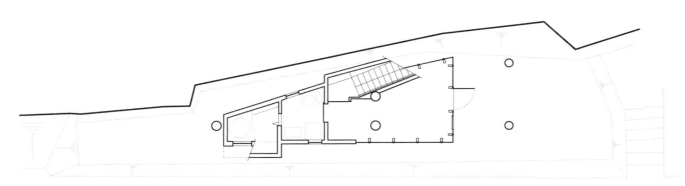

Lower floor plan

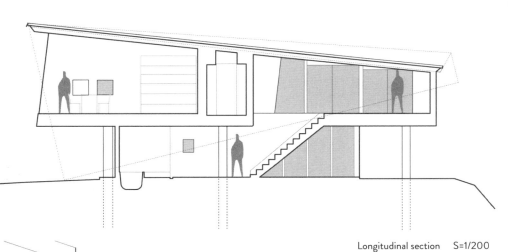

Longitudinal section　S=1/200

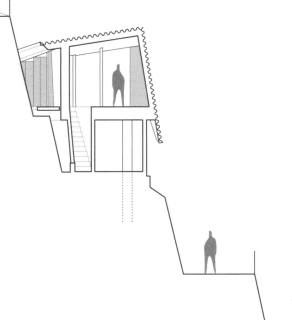

Cross section　　　S=1/200

Villa in the south of France

Atelier Barani
France
Photos © Serge Demailly

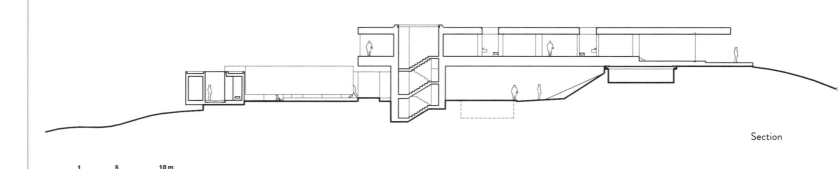

Section

1 5 10 m

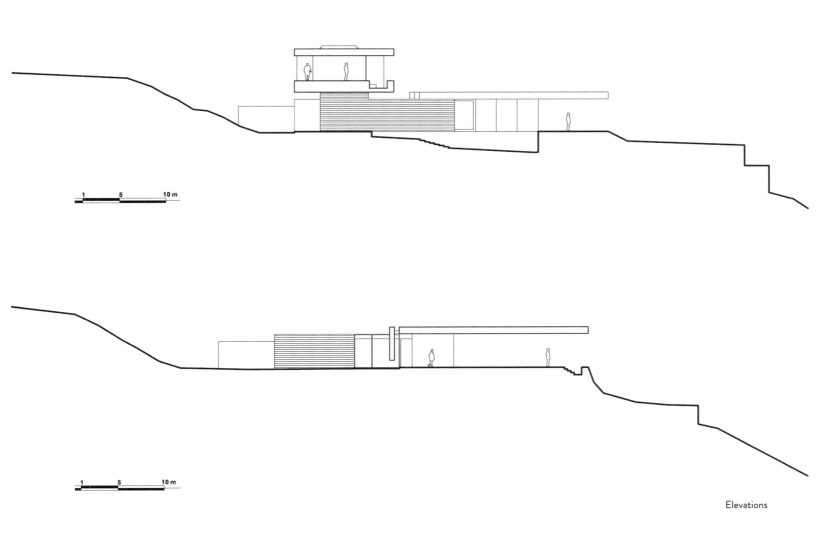

1 5 10 m

1 5 10 m

Elevations

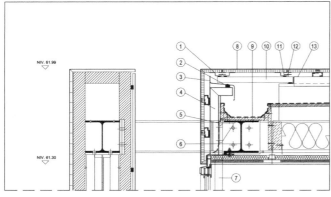

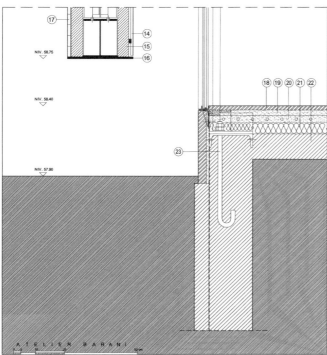

1. 40X25X2mm "Z" profile fixed to the panels
2. Wedge + fixation
3. Folded metal sheet
4. Rectangular section holder in galvanized steel 30X60 with fixing brackets aligned on the shaft PRS 500
5. PVC waterproofing membrane
6. HEA 240
7. Solid iron clamp 50X50mm
8. Panels covered with stone on alveolar structure of aluminum and epoxy
9. EP Gutter
10. 40X40 ceiling support profile
11. Plastic wedge
12. Anti-lift device
13. Profile "Z" 40X50X2mm
14. Painted POLYESTER coating
15. Cellular concrete
16. Plate
17. Stone stuck to masonry support
18. Stone cladding
19. Sealing
20. Underfloor heating
21. Isolation
22. Concrete
23. Anchorage

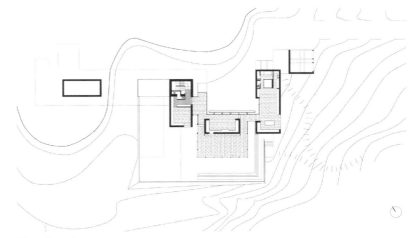

Upper floor plan

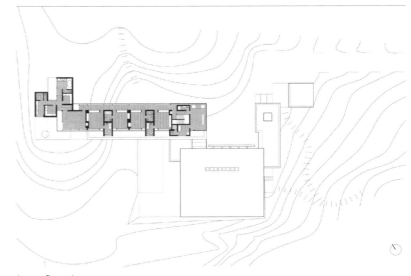

Lower floor plan

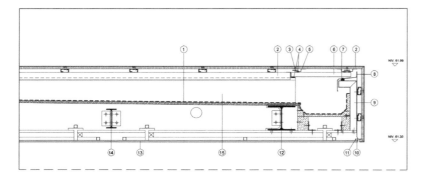

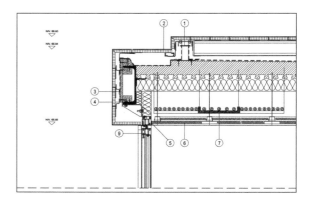

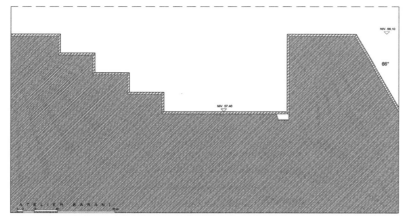

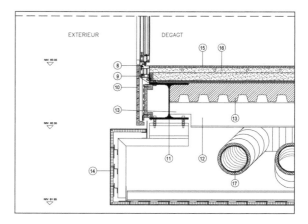

1. Waterproofing pad
2. Panels covered with stone on alveolar structure of aluminum and epoxy
3. PVC waterproofing membrane
4. Metal angle
5. Corniere alu + strip of liege (contact uncoupling carpentry)
6. Dropped acoustic ceiling
7. Wires
8. Metal edge
9. Metal joinery with thermal break + insulating glazing
10. Wood paneling - teak 22mm
11. HEA 200
12. IPE 300
13. Floor
14. Panels covered with stone on alveolar structure
15. Exotic wood floor
16. Radiant floor

1. PVC waterproofing membrane
2. 40X25X2mm "Z" profile fixed to the panels
3. Anti-lift device with rotating plate
4. Plastic fastening
5. "Z" profile 40X50X2mm
6. 40X40 ceiling support profile
7. Shim + fastened seal
8. Folded metal sheet
9. Rectangular section holder in galvanized steel 30X60 with fixing brackets aligned on the shaft PRS 500
10. 35mm POLYESTER dropped ceiling
11. Perforated sheet
12. HEA 240
13. Dropped painted POLYESTER ceiling
14. IPE 180
15. PRS 500

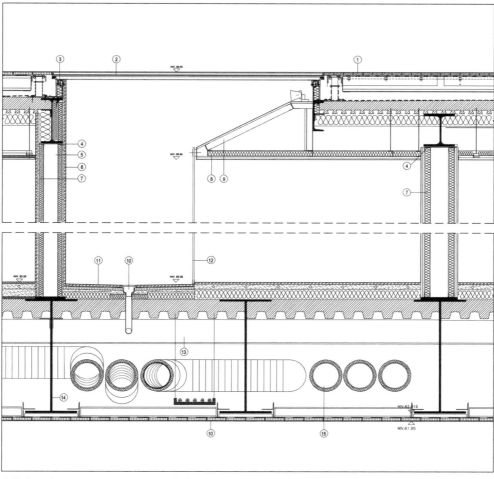

1. Teak overlay
2. Canopy 2100X2100mm
3. Metallic carpentry
4. Sound seal
5. Metal reinforcements

6. Panels covered with stone on alveolar
structure of aluminum and epoxy
7. Drywalls + insulation
8. Dropped plaster ceiling
9. Metal structure + plasterboard
dressing

10. Shower siphon
11. Stone coating
12. Shower screen - opal glazing
13. IPE 200
14. PRS 900

Residence on a vineyard

John Wardle Architects
Victoria, Australia
Photos © Trevor Mein

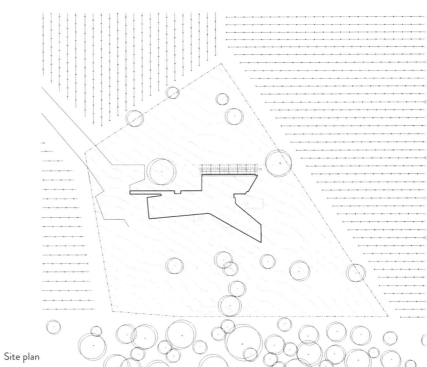

Site plan

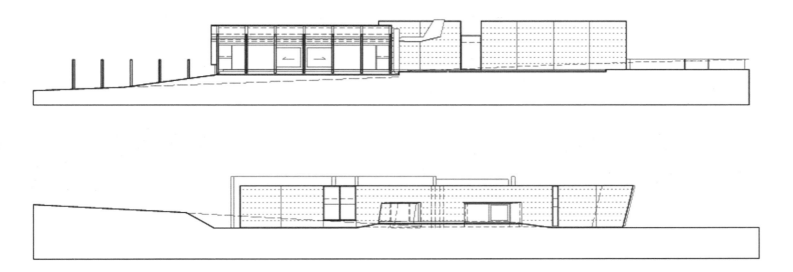

Sections

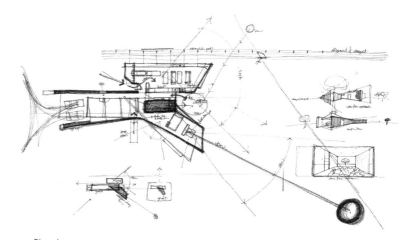

Sketch

Camouflage House

Johnsen Schmaling Architects
Green Lake, WI, USA
Photos © John Macaulay (exterior),
Kevin Miyazaki (interior)

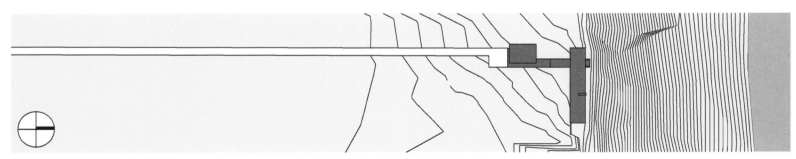

Site plan

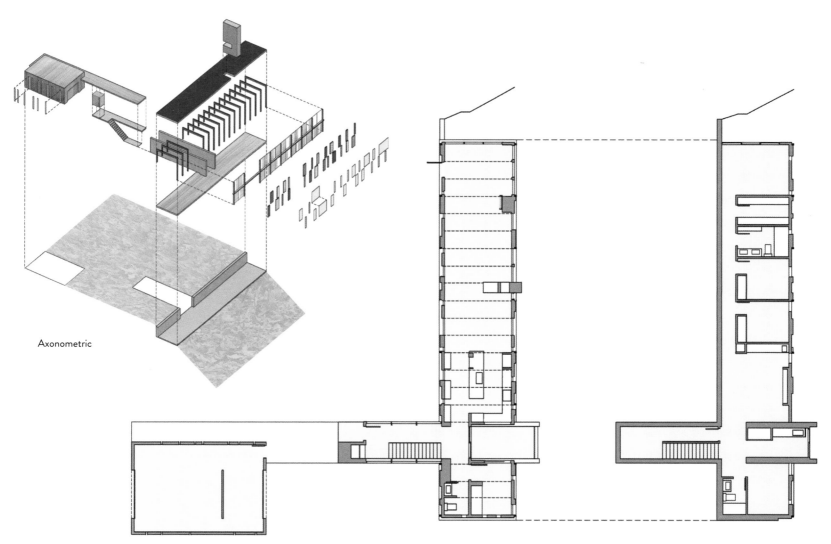

Axonometric

Floor plans

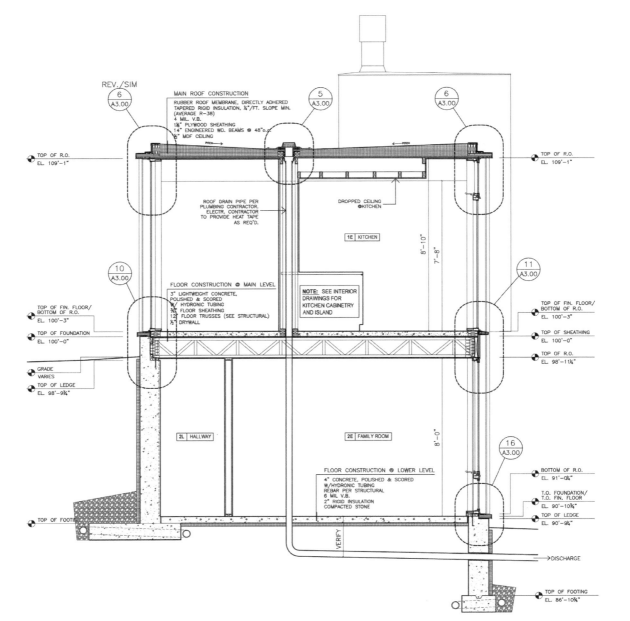

REV./SIM

6
A3.00

MAIN ROOF CONSTRUCTION
RUBBER ROOF MEMBRANE, DIRECTLY ADHERED
TAPERED RIGID INSULATION, ⅛"/FT. SLOPE MIN.
(AVERAGE R-38)
4 MIL. V.B.
1⅛" PLYWOOD SHEATHING
14" ENGINEERED WD. BEAMS @ 48"o.c.
½" MDF CEILING

5
A3.00

6
A3.00

TOP OF R.O.
EL. 109'-1"

TOP OF R.O.
EL. 109'-1"

ROOF DRAIN PIPE PER
PLUMBING CONTRACTOR.
ELECTR. CONTRACTOR
TO PROVIDE HEAT TAPE
AS REQ'D.

DROPPED CEILING
@KITCHEN

1E KITCHEN

8'-10"

7'-8"

10
A3.00

FLOOR CONSTRUCTION @ MAIN LEVEL
3" LIGHTWEIGHT CONCRETE,
POLISHED & SCORED
W/ HYDRONIC TUBING
¾" FLOOR SHEATHING
12" FLOOR TRUSSES (SEE STRUCTURAL)
½" DRYWALL

NOTE: SEE INTERIOR
DRAWINGS FOR
KITCHEN CABINETRY
AND ISLAND

11
A3.00

TOP OF FIN. FLOOR/
BOTTOM OF R.O.
EL. 100'-3"

TOP OF FIN. FLOOR/
BOTTOM OF R.O.
EL. 100'-3"

TOP OF FOUNDATION
EL. 100'-0"

TOP OF SHEATHING
EL. 100'-0"

TOP OF R.O.
EL. 98'-11¼"

GRADE
VARIES

TOP OF LEDGE
EL. 98'-9¾"

2L HALLWAY

2E FAMILY ROOM

8'-0"

16
A3.00

FLOOR CONSTRUCTION @ LOWER LEVEL
4" CONCRETE, POLISHED & SCORED
W/HYDRONIC TUBING
REBAR PER STRUCTURAL
6 MIL V.B.
2" RIGID INSULATION
COMPACTED STONE

BOTTOM OF R.O.
EL. 91'-0¼"

T.O. FOUNDATION/
T.O. FIN. FLOOR
EL. 90'-10¾"

TOP OF LEDGE
EL. 90'-9¼"

TOP OF FOOTING

VERIFY

DISCHARGE

TOP OF FOOTING
EL. 86'-10¾"

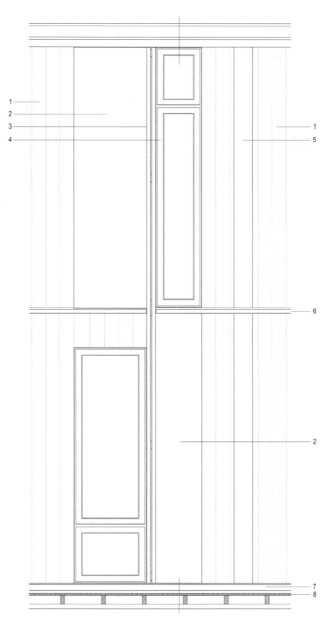

1. Vertical cedar board siding
2. Epoxy core wood veneer paneling
3. Double-layered ipe column
4. Aluminium-clad wood window
5. Ipa wall panel
6. Ipa sill
7. Aluminium sill
8. Ipa board

Barksdale Residence

Bryan Russell
Atlanta, GA, USA
Photos © Hiroyuki Oki

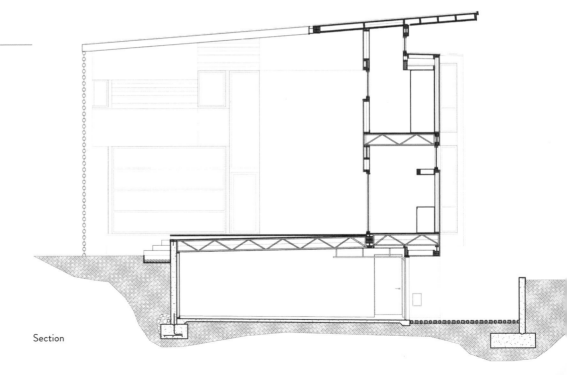

Section

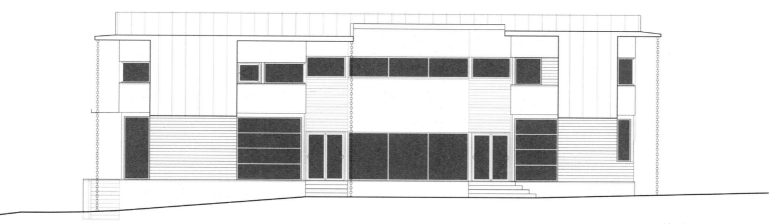

North elevation

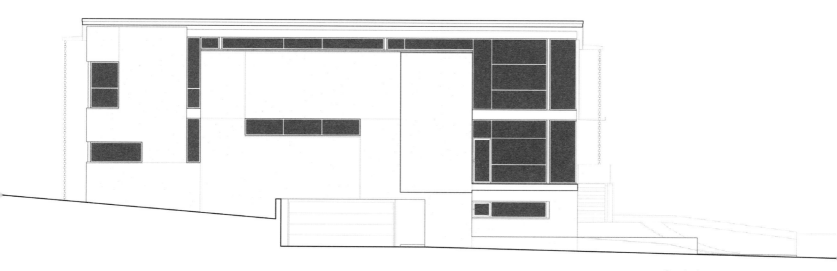

South elevation

First floor plan

Second floor plan

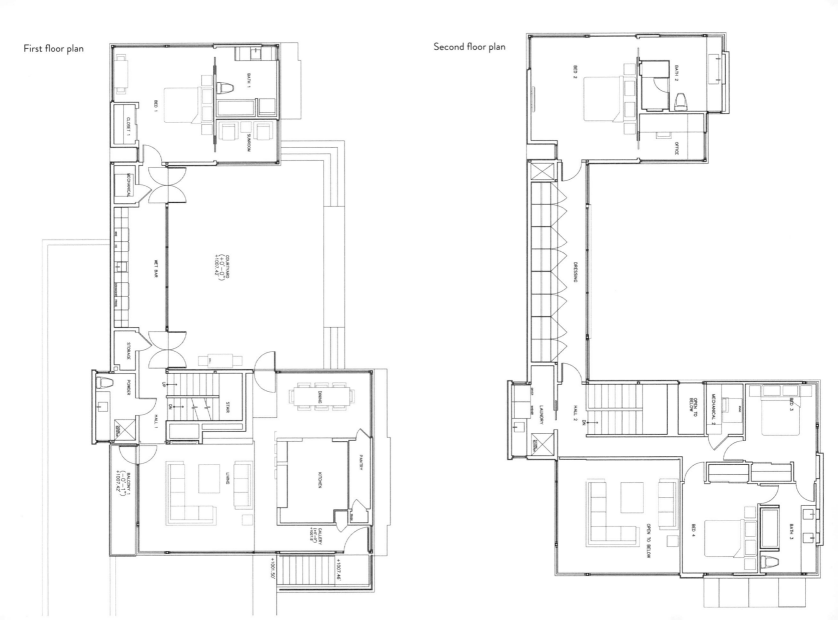

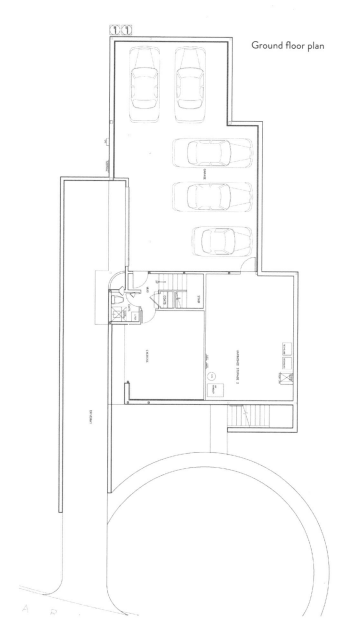

Ground floor plan

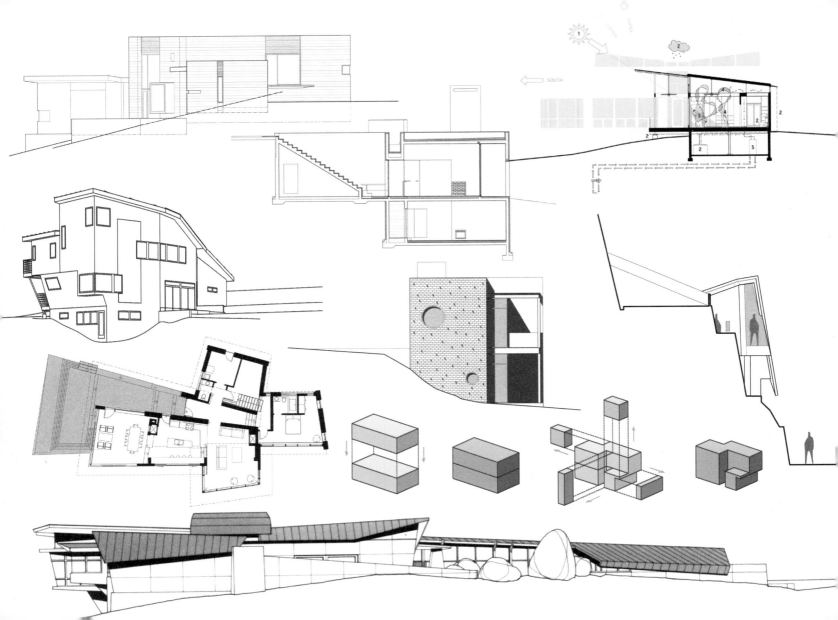

SOUTH